LOST BONANZAS
Of Western Canada

LOST BONANZAS
Of Western Canada

TRUE STORIES of LOST MINES, BURIED
or SUNKEN TREASURE and OUTLAW LOOT
from BRITISH COLUMBIA and YUKON   VOLUME 2

EDITED BY
GARNET BASQUE

VICTORIA · VANCOUVER · CALGARY

Heritage House Publishing Company Ltd.
heritagehouse.ca

LIBRARY AND ARCHIVES CANADA CATALOGUING IN PUBLICATION

Lost bonanzas of Western Canada
First ed. by T.W. Paterson.
Includes bibliographical references and index.

ISBN 13: 978-1-895811-40-7 (v. 1)—ISBN 13: 978-1-895811-86-5 (v. 2)
ISBN 10: 1-895811-40-6 (v. 1)—ISBN 10: 1-895811-86-4 (v. 2)

1. Treasure-trove—Canada, Western. 2. Treasure-trove—Canada, Northern.
3. Canada, Western—History. 4. Canada, Northern—History. I. Basque, Garnet.
II. Paterson, T.W. (Thomas William), 1943–

FC3206.P37 1996   971.2'02   C95-910256-6   F1060.P37 1996

Photo Credits: Anderson, Irvin: 105. B.C. Government: 81 (*top*). B.C. Archives: 8, 14, 17, 24, 37 (*bottom*), 48, 60, 69, 74, 78, 80, 82, 94–95, 96, 108 (*inset*), 110, 111, 114, 120 (*bottom*), 124, 128 (*bottom*), 131. Barlee, N.L.: 115. Basque, Garnet: Front cover, 4, 12, 18, 22, 23, 38, 46–47, 50, 54, 59, 62, 63, 77, 81 (*bottom*), 89, 97 (*main*), 100, 101, 112 (*top*), 113, 116, 117, 120 (top). Clark, Cecil: 141. CPR Archives: 35. Dunn, Mrs. I.: 121. Fenske, Mike: 19 (*bottom*), 26, 27, 30. Glenbow Archives: 88 (*bottom*). McKelvie, B.A.: 134. National Archives: 72, 84, 90. Oliphant, John: 132, 136, 138, 139. Sunfire Archives: 19 (*top*), 33, 34, 37 (*top*), 42, 55, 83, 85, 88 (*top*), 97 (*inset*), 108–109, 112 (*bottom*), 125, 126 (*top*). U.S. Signal Corps: 99.

Heritage House acknowledges the financial support for its publishing program from the Government of Canada through the Canada Book Fund (CBF), Canada Council for the Arts, and the Province of British Columbia through the British Columbia Arts Council and the Book Publishing Tax Credit.

Canadian Heritage   Patrimoine canadien   The Canada Council for the Arts | Le Conseil des Arts du Canada   BRITISH COLUMBIA ARTS COUNCIL

Printed in China through Colorcraft Ltd, Hong Kong.

19 18 17 16 15 4 5 6 7 8

CONTENTS

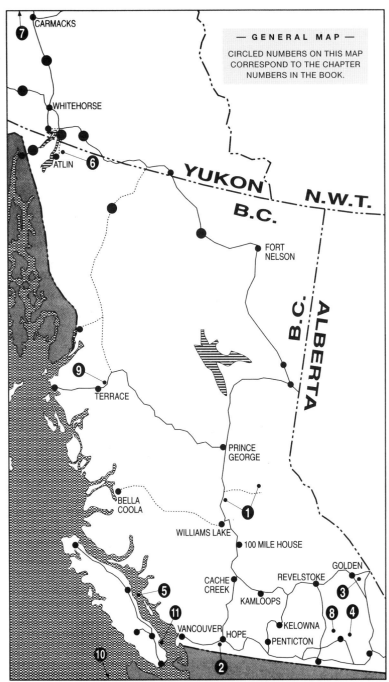

CHAPTER 1

THE LOST DRAGON MINE

*This mine was first discovered by three Swedes in 1864. When they aban-
doned it in search of richer goldfields, it was three decades before it was
re-discovered. Unfortunately, the new discoverer was killed before he
could work the mine and it has been eagerly sought ever since.*

THE gold miners who participated in the Fraser River gold rush in
1858 were predominately Americans from the dwindling mines
of California. Although they discovered plenty of gold along the
Fraser, it was rather fine. As a result, many continued to pick and pan
their way north in search of coarser gold. Late in 1859, coarse gold was
discovered at the mouth of the Quesnel River, and by the summer of
1860 some 600 miners were successfully employed there, recovering $10
to $25 per day. That fall a handful of miners constructed rafts and boats
and penetrated the main and north branches of the Quesnel River. When
they returned in November with bags of gold, the news revived the fal-
tering Fraser River gold rush by focusing attention on a new, albeit
remote and unexplored region.

The town of Quesnel Forks, which sprang up in the centre of the
new discoveries and once boasted a population of over 5,000, served as a
base for miners still not content with the local goldfields. When four of
these adventurers, John Rose, Ben McDonald, "Doc" Keithley and
George Weaver, discovered Keithley Creek about 20 miles from Quesnel
Forks, it altered the course of Cariboo history.

In 1861, William Dietz discovered gold on Williams Creek. From
there the miners branched out, and virtually all streams within a 20-mile
radius were found to be gold bearing. In the summer of 1862, a sailor
named Billy Barker entered the Cariboo. Unable to find unstaked
ground, he decided to try below the canyon on Williams Creek, much to
everyone's amusement. However, when Barker struck extremely rich
pay dirt at the 52-foot mark of his shaft, others turned their attention to
the area. Among them was John "Cariboo" Cameron, whose claim
became the richest in the Cariboo. Around the claims of Cameron and
Barker grew the boomtowns of Cameronton and Barkerville, the latter
being declared "the largest community west of Chicago and north of San

Francisco," and heralded as the "gold capital of the world."

The Cariboo proved to be of almost unbelievable richness, with numerous individual claims yielding fortunes in the precious metal. The Caledonia and Neversweat claims on Williams Creek yielded $750,000 and $120,000 respectively; Butcher's Bench ($125,000), Forest Rose ($480,000), and Prairie Flower ($100,000) being but a few others.

By 1865, although the creeks were still yielding more than $3,000,000 annually, the shallow diggings were becoming exhausted. With the day of the individual miner coming to an end, most prospectors began searching for new discoveries. Eventually strikes in the Omineca, Peace, Cassiar and Atlin districts were explored and mined.

ORIGINAL LEGEND

Deriving its name from Dragon Mountain, an old and weathered mountain two miles east of Quesnel, this lost placer is also known as the Lost Swede's Mine or the Lost Frenchman Mine. The primary source of information concerning the Lost Dragon Mine would appear to be an article written by Art Downs in 1950,[1] subsequent articles merely being variations of that account.

Downs apparently obtained his information from Charlie Coplin and Robert Barlow, two miners who followed the lost mine's history. According to Barlow, the mine was first discovered by three Swedes in 1864. The men averaged about $12 a day, which they cashed in at Bob Goudie's small trading post at Quesnel. With other Cariboo claims yielding 70 to 400 ounces a day, and with the high cost of provisions then prevailing in the Cariboo, $12 a day to the man was not considered very worthwhile. Thus, when news of a rich placer strike in the Peace

1 Art Downs was editor and publisher of the *Cariboo and Northwest Digest* in which the article appeared.

The discovery made by Billy Barker (left) in 1862 led to the foundation of Barkerville, shown below in 1865.

River country reached the Quesnel area, the three Swedes packed their gear and headed north.

The creek lay forgotten and abandoned for three decades, until, in 1893, a rugged trapper named Ben La Roche stumbled across the old placer workings. La Roche was brushing out a trap line on Dragon Mountain when he came upon a deep gorge which he decided to examine for mink signs. According to Downs: "He went down a steep side-hill but the area didn't seem favourable for trapping and he started to leave. Then he saw what appeared to be placer workings, long since abandoned. Further investigation turned up two mattock heads and three shovel blades, the handles rotted or burned away. And nearby, close to the canyon wall, was the remains of a cabin. The shack had burned years before, but he could still see where the earth had been banked against the logs to keep out the winter cold."

Excited by the discovery, La Roche worked the claim for eight days before heading back to Quesnel to relate the news to his old friend Jimmy Shepherd. As luck would have it, Shepherd was about to leave the Cariboo to return to the bedside of his ailing mother in England when La Roche met him. Although Shepherd was in a hurry, he agreed to return to La Roche's cabin with him. Once inside, "La Roche spread a newspaper on the table and emptied the contents of a fairly large buckskin pouch. Shepherd looked at the paper and gasped. Before him was about 18 ounces of gold, among it some fairly large nuggets." Shepherd, an experienced Cariboo prospector, later stated that the gold "was different from anything he had seen," adding that the "smallest pieces were the size of cracked wheat."[2]

Without providing details of where the discovery had been made, La Roche explained how he had accidentally stumbled on the old placer workings, stating "I wanted to test the workings for myself, so I climbed the canyon wall, dropped two large poplars and rolled the butt ends down the slope. I hewed sluice-boxes out of the logs, made willow riffles, and chopped handles for a spade and mattock."[3] By nightfall La Roche had recovered two ounces, and in eight days, the 18 ounces gleaming on the table before them. La Roche went on to relate how he believed that this was the Lost Swedes' Mine, suggesting that they must "have left before they hit pay dirt." La Roche went on to explain that he was a trapper, not a miner, and he was willing to give Shepherd a full share for his help.

Shepherd was willing, but he first had to go to England to visit his sick mother. This delay did not appear to bother La Roche, who said he would wait for his return. But, as with many treasure stories, fate tragically intervened. On May 10, 1894, the very day Shepherd returned from England, La Roche was killed by a frisky horse. With his death went the

2 *Ibid.*
3 *Ibid.*

secret to the lost mine. Undeterred, and spurred on by the memory of those coarse nuggets, Shepherd tried in vain to locate the site.

Four years later a prospector named Blair was travelling along the Quesnel River trail from Quesnel Forks en route to Quesnel. Upon reaching a point a little north of Beaver Creek, Blair decided to take a short-cut over the mountains to the old Cariboo Road. As he was crossing the mountains, he suddenly stumbled across some old placer workings and found the foundations of an old cabin. With a rusty gold pan he found at the site, he tested the creek. The prospects were excellent. Blair then rushed to Quesnel for supplies, then headed back into the area. Unfortunately, although he searched until freeze-up, Blair was unable to relocate the creek again.

When the frustrated Blair returned to Quesnel, he revealed the reason for his mysterious trip. Relating the information about his discovery, he described the old workings as "...shallow, only five or six feet of gravel covering bed-rock. Lying around the area were pieces of gum rubbers, old cans, and rusty mining tools. Then near the wall of the canyon he saw the unmistakable imprint of the bottom logs of a cabin."[4]

Everyone who heard the story was convinced that Blair had re-discovered the Lost Dragon Mine, and a rush quickly ensued. But, despite extensive searches throughout the area, the site of Blair's discovery could not be located.

Two years later, in 1900, a man by the name of Murray arrived at Shepherd's Ranch, a favourite stopping place along the Cariboo Road. During his stay Murray told Shepherd that an old Indian at Quesnel had told him about "a rich gold deposit about a three hour hike from the Cariboo road." The Indian promised to show Murray the spot if he could not locate it by himself. After hunting unsuccessfully for some days, Murray returned to Quesnel to locate the Indian. Unfortunately, fate had intervened once again, the Indian having died the day before he got there.

The lost mine was revived a decade later when a party of men stopped in to visit Shepherd. Among them were Robert Barlow and a big Swede. When the topic of the lost mine came up, the big Swede became very interested, and soon afterward he headed into the hills. When Barlow chanced to meet the big Swede in Vancouver in 1911, he inquired about his treasure-hunting trip. The Swede related how he had encountered a deep canyon, but had found no signs of any placer operations, and the creek bed itself was dry. Barlow concluded that the Swede had stumbled upon the mysterious canyon, but had not been able to locate the precise site because of heavy overgrowth.

For 50 years the secret of the Lost Dragon Mine remained a tantalizing mystery. Finally, in June 1951, Albert Bresette and Ernie Floyd, both veteran prospectors from the Matson Creek area, resolved to solve the

4 *Ibid.*

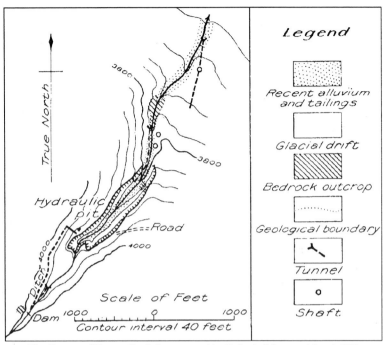

The diagram of Dragon Creek that appeared in Geological Survey, Memoir 149.

puzzle once and for all. Heading into the hills they came to a promising site. "While prospecting up a small creek, due east of Kersley, they stumbled and fell over a mound of rocks, dislodging a portion of the moss that covered them. This revealed that the rocks had been laid in position, a sure sign that a prospector had been at work."[5]

But was it the Lost Dragon Mine? Based on the samples taken by Bresette and Floyd, they determined that, if it was, "the early reports were grossly exaggerated."

INVESTIGATING THE FACTS

As interesting and intriguing as this lost mine appears upon first reading, there is, alas, almost no supportive evidence. The lost mine is supposed to be located near Dragon Mountain, about two miles east of Quesnel. Yet none of the *Minister of Mines* reports record any gold mining activity having taken place in that region in even a superficial way. None of the creeks in the area are noted gold producers, and no reference to any of the individuals are found in the *Minister of Mines* for that region. If the supposed location of the lost Dragon Creek mine was incorrect, however, many pieces of the puzzle would begin to fit together.

As it turns out, the Cariboo region has *two* Dragon mountains and *two* Dragon creeks. The first Dragon Mountain and Dragon Creek are

5 *Ibid.*

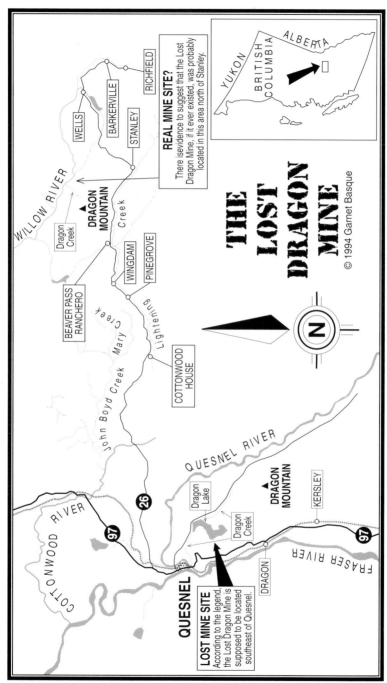

THE LOST DRAGON MINE

© 1994 Garnet Basque

REAL MINE SITE?

There is evidence to suggest that the Lost Dragon Mine, if it ever existed, was probably located in this area north of Stanley.

LOST MINE SITE

According to the legend, the Lost Dragon Mine is supposed to be located southeast of Quesnel.

WILLOW RIVER

WELLS

BARKERVILLE

STANLEY

RICHFIELD

DRAGON MOUNTAIN

Dragon Creek

Creek

BEAVER PASS RANCHERO

WINGDAM

PINEGROVE

Mary Creek

John Boyd Creek

Lightening Creek

COTTONWOOD HOUSE

QUESNEL RIVER

DRAGON MOUNTAIN

Dragon Lake

Dragon Creek

KERSLEY

DRAGON

FRASER RIVER

QUESNEL

COTTONWOOD RIVER

26

97

97

YUKON

ALBERTA

BRITISH COLUMBIA

located about two miles southeast of Quesnel. This has always been the suggested lost mine site. The second location, however, is considerable more favourable in a number of ways.

Located about two miles north of the Quesnel-Barkerville road, the second Dragon Mountain is about four miles northwest of the ghost town of Stanley. Dragon Creek runs southeast from the mountain and empties into the Willow River. Researching this area as the possible lost placer site has produced some tantalizing clues. For example, according to W.A. Johnston and W.L. Uglow,[6] this Dragon Creek was ". . .named after a French Canadian (a Mr. Bourassa) who, because of his great strength and fighting abilities was nicknamed 'Dragon'." Their report goes on to state: "Prospecting and mining work on Dragon creek have been carried on almost continuously since the early days and a great deal of work has been done. One-eyed Davis, who also had a claim on Williams creek, was one of the first to mine the creek. The creek was drifted from above the canyon to above the present head of the hydraulic pit (1926). A tunnel was started about 400 feet below the present dam and struck bedrock not far from the dam. The workings are said to have been abandoned at the time of the Cassiar excitement in 1874. A long tunnel near the forks of the creek in the upper part was run by Otto Muller in recent years, but bedrock was not reached."[7] The gold of Dragon Creek, noted for its coarse, nuggety character, and for its fineness or purity, assayed about $19 an ounce.

There are four intriguing similarities between the original lost mine legend and this brief excerpt from *Memoir 149*. First, one name for the Lost Dragon Mine, as stated, was the Lost Frenchman Mine. As has been shown above, the second Dragon Mountain was named after a French Canadian. Second, the Dragon Creek of legend and the second Dragon Creek both have a canyon. Third, the legend states that the mine was first worked by Swedes and abandoned during a gold rush to the Peace River Country. *Memoir 149* states that this second Dragon Creek was also worked early, then abandoned during the Cassiar gold rush. Fourth; is the Murray of legend supposed to be the Muller of fact? Granted the name of the Frenchman in both cases is different, and the other pieces of the puzzle are not precise fits, but are they mere coincidence? If they are, here are a couple more "coincidences."

According to the legend "a man named Blair" was involved in a search for the lost mine in 1894. Even though the years are different, is it simply coincidence that the only reference to a Blair in the *Minister of Mines* reports for the entire Cariboo region states that in 1886, "James Blair lost his life by the bursting in of water and gravel from the channel into the bedrock `drive'," on the Nason claim on Upper Antler Creek?

6 W.A. Johnston and W.L. Uglow, *Placer and Vein Gold Deposits of Barkerville, Cariboo District, British Columbia*, (Ottawa, Geological Survey, Memoir 149, 1926, p. 153).
7 *Ibid*, pp. 154-155.

(Above) A general view of Stanley, also known as Van Winkle. The second Dragon Creek is located four miles northwest of this ghost town.
(Below) The Stanley Hotel, Stanley, c1907.

This is only 10 miles from the second Dragon Creek.

It is also interesting to note that the *B.C. Directory* for 1885 lists a miner named John Blair under the Stanley subheading, but gives his actual address as Dragon Creek. As pointed out earlier, the second Dragon Creek is only four miles northwest of the Stanley town-site. If John Blair was working the first Dragon Creek, near Quesnel, would it not seem more likely that he would live in Quesnel?

Another coincidence is that, although there is no Jimmy Shepherd mentioned in any of the *Minister of Mines* reports, there is a reference to an E.C. Shepherd in the 1892 report: "The only discovery made in the district this season, which may be regarded as entirely new, was that of Mr. E.C. Shepherd and partner, on a small stream which flows into Antler Creek, and is now known as Shepherd Creek. The discovery was made near the source of the creek in Downie Pass, two and a half miles east of Williams Creek meadows. As the gold is of a coarse character and well washed, hopes are entertained that the discovery may lead to something important."[8]

Meanwhile, referring again to the 1926 *Geological Survey*, we find a reference to a "John" Shepherd, who, with John Duffy, discovered gold on Pine Creek in 1894. Shepherd Creek, incidentally, is the main branch of Pine Creek.

SUMMARY AND CONCLUSION

We know for a fact that there was a great deal of gold mining activity surrounding the Dragon Mountain nearest Stanley, while there is not a single reference to gold in the vicinity of the Dragon Mountain nearest Quesnel. Furthermore, there are references to a Frenchman, a man named Blair and a man named Shepherd, all within 10 miles of the Dragon Creek near Stanley, while absolutely none are found in connection with the Dragon Creek near Quesnel. Granted, these references are not precise, nor are they indisputable, but information pertaining to lost mines rarely is. Yet, does it not seem odd that we can find no similar clues near the Dragon Mountain of legend?

A great deal more research is obviously necessary before a definitive conclusion can be reached, but from what I have gathered to date, I believe the lost mine, if it exists at all, must be located on the Dragon Creek northwest of Stanley. It is interesting to note that in the 1870s "...a tunnel was started near the junction of Dragon creek and Willow river and is said to have been run through very bad ground for over 1,000 feet up Dragon creek, with the object of reaching the deep lower part of the creek, but bedrock was never reached."[9]

Other attempts to locate an "old channel" also failed. Did these failed attempts to reach bedrock or find the old channel, often referred to as a "lost" channel, give rise to the lost mine story? Who can say for certain. What is known, however, is that quite often legend is based on fact. The facts presented pertaining to the Dragon Creek near Stanley, I would suggest, are more than ample fodder upon which active minds could develop a lost mine story. Somewhere along the way, in the telling and retelling, I think the mine's location became confused with the Dragon Mountain near Quesnel. But we may never know.   ❀

---

8 *B.C. Minister of Mines Report*, 1892, p. 527.
9 W.A. Johnston and W.L. Uglow, *op. cit.*, p. 155.

Chapter 2

THE FORGOTTEN MINES OF SILVER PEAK MOUNTAIN

Do rich silver mines lie forgotten and abandoned in the mountains just south of Hope, B.C.? According to the story, the mines, first discovered in 1868, yielded some exceedingly rich ore until the mines closed in 1874. But is was not a lack of ore that forced the mines to close, but rather a combination of bad management, lack of transportation and litigation.

ACCORDING to most reports, the mines on Silver Peak Mountain were rich, fabulously rich. Unfortunately, the mines appear to have also been jinxed, for four of the principals involved with them met with tragic and untimely deaths.

Most of the information pertaining to the silver mines is contained in three articles. The first, written by V.G. St. George, appeared in the February, 1901 edition of the *B.C. Mining Record*. Next comes an article written by Arthur S. Williamson that appeared in the Vancouver *Daily Province* on December 16, 1921. Finally, two articles were written by David Loughnan. Basically identical, one appeared in the Victoria *Daily Colonist* on July 5, 1924. The second appeared in the *Daily Province*. These sources, with minor differences, all relate essentially the same information, although each article emphasizes a different aspect of the story. St. George's account, for example, concentrates itself mostly with the richness of the mines; Williamson, who re-discovered the mine in 1921, is more concerned with that discovery, while Loughnan's treatment is more general and all-encompassing. The story that follows is a careful blending of these three accounts, substantiated or clarified by primary sources such as the *B.C. Minister of Mines* reports and the Victoria *Daily Colonist*.

While all three accounts agree that the first discovery was made by an Indian of the Emery Bar Reservation while out hunting goat, there is disagreement as to the name of the Indian and date of his discovery. St. George states that the discovery was made by "George Wil-willuts, in 1870." Williamson and Loughnan give the Indian's name as "Peter Emery" and list the date of discovery as "1868." While this discrepancy is not important to the outcome of the story, it does warrant some investigation.

Since Loughnan's account was the last written, and draws a lot of its information from Williamson's article, I think we can safely assume that he merely repeated information published in Williamson's article. Nor was he the only one. In the Canada *Geological Survey, Memoir 139,* dated 1924, C.E. Cairnes, quoting directly from Williamson's article, states: "It was first discovered by an Indian, Peter Emery, while hunting goat in 1868." Mining Engineer A.D. Davis repeats the same information in the *B.C. Minister of Mines* report for 1924 when he states: "This property. . . was located in 1868." Although Davis does not credit Williamson as his source for this information, he does add: "Identified with the new company now developing the Eureka-Victoria is Arthur S. Williamson and G.D.B. Turner, of Vancouver." This can leave little doubt that Williamson was the source for all subsequent references to Peter Emery and 1868. Thus we need only consider the accounts of St. George and Williamson.

The *B.C. Minister of Mines* report for 1874 states that the Eureka silver mine was "discovered about 1871," which would tend to agree with St. George. Also, since no written references can be found relating to any date earlier that 1871, as will be seen as this story unfolds, it must be considered very unlikely that the discovery was made in 1868. As for the name of the actual discoverer, I give more credibility to St. George for a number of reasons. First, his report was the earliest to appear, in 1901. Second, the *B.C. Mining Record,* like the *B.C. Minister of Mines,* served to record the mining events of the province. Williamson's account was not written for another 20 years. And even he admits that he was drawn to search for the "lost" mine by rumours. It is possible that by this time the discoverer's name had been forgotten, but someone, confusing the fact that he was from "Emery" Bar, thought his last name was Emery. In any event, until official records surface to prove otherwise, I will assume that

Pay day on Emery Creek in the 1880s. George Wil-willuts, the Indian credited with discovering the silver mine, lived near here.

HOPE

HOPE
MOUNTAIN

SILVER
LAKE

Eureka Creek

6,806

SILVER
PEAK

ISOLILLOCK
PEAK

Sowerby Creek

MOUNT
STONEMAN

SILVERHOPE CREEK

N

(Above) This sketch of the Eureka Silver mine's buildings and crew appeared in the Canadian Illustrated News in 1872.
(Opposite page) This 1990 view of Silver Peak Mountains was taken from the south.
(Opposite page, inset) A general map of the area.
(Below right) Mike Fenske stands in the mine adit on Silver Peak in Mountain in 1993.

George Wil-willuts was the discoverer.

After his discovery, Wil-willuts took some of the float back to Yale where he showed it to Thomas Schooley (incorrectly spelled Chooley by Williamson and Loughnan). A carefree, good-natured, clean-cut carpenter from Pennsylvania, Schooley, nicknamed "Happy Tom," is said to have given Wil-willuts a rifle to lead him and George Dunbar back to the site. It is also stated that Schooley made a coffin for the Indian's wife, who died shortly thereafter. St. George makes no mention of the coffin, but he claims that, according to local tradition, Wil-willuts never received the rifle either.

After an arduous trip to the mountaintop, it took only a brief examination to convince Schooley and Dunbar that they were standing on a

rich silver mine, and they promptly staked the Eureka and Victoria claims, which became the first Crown-granted quartz claims in B.C. According to Alfred Selwyn's report for the Canada *Geological Survey* (1871-72), the proprietors valued their claims at $300,000. "Difficulty of transport, the high price of labour, and the want of requisite capital have, however, hitherto prevented its development."

Lacking development capital, Schooley and Dunbar began to search for wealthy investors, and in September, 1871, the Eureka Silver Mining Company was formed with a capital of $150,000 divided into 3,000 shares worth $50 each. Some of the major shareholders included: George Dietz, an original Cariboo miner and owner of the stage line from Yale to Barkerville; H. Nelson, who later became lieutenant-governor of the province; Sewell P. Moody, after whom Moodyville was named, who built the first sawmill on Burrard Inlet; Frank Garesche, a former Wells Fargo employee who was running his own private bank in Victoria; R.P. Rithet, James Van Bremer and J.C. Hughes. According to Loughnan, Schooley and Dunbar were bought out for $80,000—a fortune in 1871!

The biggest obstacle facing the mining company was the inaccessibility of its mines, situated over 5,000 feet up the mountain. Gradually a 10-mile-long pack trail connected Hope with the mines, the last four of which were consisted of steep zigzags. All food, supplies and machinery had to be packed in. Once ore was mined, it was packed to the bottom of the mountain by Indians, and from there taken to Hope on the backs of mules. From Hope, steamers transported the ore to Victoria, from where it was transshipped to London or San Francisco by sea.

The first recorded shipment appeared in the January 23, 1872 issue of the Victoria *Colonist,* which noted that eight tons of ore were to be shipped to San Francisco the following day for a "practical test." The May 5 edition reported that assays revealed $395 worth of silver to the ton. On September 26 the *Colonist* notes that: "S.P. Moody, who returned from San Francisco yesterday, brings a very encouraging report from the three or four tons of silver ore which he took down. The ore was sold at $230 per ton, while from 240 lbs, two silver bricks worth $71.32 in silver and $6.42 in gold were extracted. . . ." A month later, on October 29, the *Colonist* stated that the assays from the Victoria silver mine's Van Bremer ledge assayed as high as $2,400 in silver and $40 in gold to the ton, and that the ore would probably average out at $500. At the time of this report, 10 tons of ore was at New Westminster waiting to be shipped to Swansea, while another 23 tons was about to be shipped to San Francisco.

Other primary sources confirm the richness of the mines. The *Geological Survey's* report for 1873-74 states: "A yellowish decomposed veinstone brought by Mr. Richardson from Hope in British Columbia, was assayed and gave at the rate of 271.48 oz. of silver to the ton of 2,000 lbs."

The B.C. *Minister of Mines* report for 1874 provides even more information:

"The first lead, called the Eureka mine, crops out about 5,000 feet above the river level, is well defined, four to seven feet in thickness and has been traced 3,000 feet. A tunnel has been driven into this lead 190 feet. The ore is described as argentiferous gray copper, and has yielded under assay from $20 to $1,050 worth of silver to the ton.

"During the same time the above lead was being worked, another about 300 feet distant was discovered. This lead is of a far more valuable character, and is called the Van Bremer Mine.

"The ore is described as chloride of silver, and has yielded under assay from $25 to $2,403 of silver per ton of rock. A quantity of the outcrop sold at San Francisco at $420 per ton. This lead is distinctly traceable for half a mile.

"Although a company has been formed for working these lodes, no works of any importance have been undertaken. It is however, rumoured that when the company have matured their plans, working of the lodes will be vigorously prosecuted."

Then tragedies, although not directly related to the mines themselves, began to plague the operations. The first tragedy involved Thomas Schooley. Back in the fall of 1871, when Schooley visited Victoria looking for investors, he had been introduced to Henry Forman, a former alderman from James Bay. Forman became interested in the wealthy mine owner and invited him to his home on St. Lawrence Street. There, Schooley met Forman's young daughter Ellen, recently arrived from England. Schooley was in his mid-40s at the time, but despite the fact that Ellen was about 20 years younger, the two fell in love. Within a few weeks the couple were wed "amid the blare of trumpets, the glare of Chinese lanterns and the popping of champagne corks." But, if the wedding was a festive occasion, the honeymoon and life after marriage apparently was anything but harmonious.

With Schooley's new-found wealth, the couple went to San Francisco for an expensive honeymoon. But, instead of happiness, the couple began to quarrel almost immediately. Three reasons have been put forth for Schooley's sudden change of temperament from a care-free, fun-loving individual to a surly wife-beating fiend. Loughnan claims that Tom was jealous of his wife and was not convinced that she loved him. Cecil Clark, a Victoria policeman who later became involved in the case, quoting some unspecified source, said that Tom "suspected his father-in-law of having designs on his money." Clark himself suggested that "Schooley's bad business judgement was the cause. Tom started out as if he had all the money in the world, but a succession of bad investments dwindled his funds. He became increasingly surly and suspicious, seeking more and more consolation from the bottle." For the record, the *Colonist,* which covered the tragedy in detail, does not provide any suggestions as to the underlying problem.

After the honeymoon in San Francisco, the couple returned to Victo-

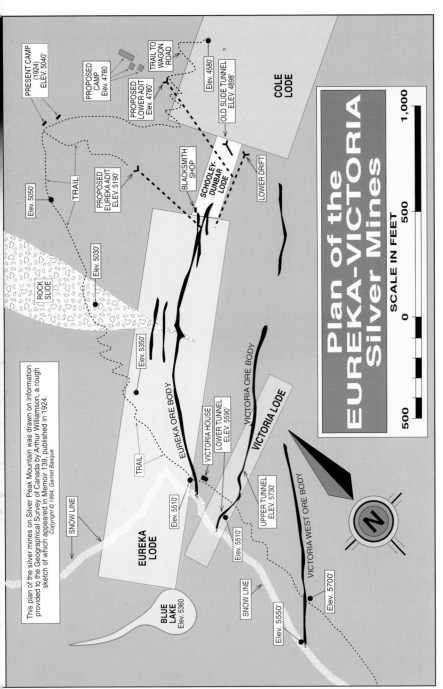

Plan of the EUREKA-VICTORIA Silver Mines

SCALE IN FEET

500   0   500   1,000

This plan of the silver mines on Silver Peak Mountain was drawn on information provided to the Geographical Survey of Canada by Arthur Williamson, a rough sketch of which appeared in Memoir 139, published in 1924.
Copyright © 1994, Garnet Basque

PRESENT CAMP (1924) ELEV. 5040'

PROPOSED CAMP Elev. 4780'

PROPOSED LOWER ADIT Elev. 4780'

TRAIL TO WAGON ROAD

Elev. 4580'

OLD SLIDE TUNNEL ELEV. 4898'

COLE LODE

Elev. 5050'

TRAIL

PROPOSED EUREKA ADIT ELEV. 5190'

BLACKSMITH SHOP

SCHOOLEY-DUNBAR LODE

LOWER DRIFT

Elev. 5030'

ROCK SLIDE

Elev. 5350'

EUREKA ORE BODY

VICTORIA ORE BODY

VICTORIA HOUSE

LOWER TUNNEL ELEV. 5590'

VICTORIA LODE

TRAIL

Elev. 5510'

EUREKA LODE

UPPER TUNNEL ELEV. 5730'

VICTORIA WEST ORE BODY

Elev. 5510'

SNOW LINE

SNOW LINE

BLUE LAKE Elev. 5360'

Elev. 5550'

Elev. 5700'

N

ria, sharing the Forman home. Although a child was born in due time, its birth did nothing to settle the problems facing Tom. As the months passed, his distrust and cruelty to his wife only intensified.

The situation culminated with a cold-blooded murder on Thursday, January 22, 1874. For several days prior to the tragedy, Schooley had been drinking freely and had been abusing his wife and Mrs. Forman. One night, Mrs. Forman later testified, he moved his trunks out and demanded his wife leave with him. When she refused, he produced a revolver and threatened to kill them both. On Wednesday evening Tom threatened to horsewhip his wife. On the day of

(Above right) Even 4x4 vehicles can't navigate past the lower portion of trail.
(Below) Boulder strewn Sowerby Creek, south of the base of Silver Peak Mountain.

the murder, he stayed in the house all day drinking port wine.

When Henry Forman arrived home that evening, "he found Schooley, still in his cups, abusive and threatening." Mrs. Forman, in an attempt to avoid further confrontations, had set her husband's dinner in the kitchen, which was connected to the dining-room by four steps. As Henry was about to eat, Tom threw a picture down the steps. Henry then followed Tom to his bedroom where he "remonstrated with him" briefly, then returned to his dinner. As he was just lifting a piece of meat to his mouth with a fork, Schooley opened the door behind him, and from the top step, fired a revolver. The bullet tore through Henry's right-hand, "struck the table at which the doomed man was seated, gouging out a piece of the wood," and then buried itself in the wall.

Sewell Moody, one of the original partners in the silver mines.

Wounded, Forman jumped up and bolted for the back door. Before he could escape, however, Schooley fired a second time. According to a later post mortem examination made by Dr. Helmcken, and sworn to under oath, the fatal bullet entered a little below the right shoulder blade and exited on the left breast a little below the left sternum. Now fatally wounded, Forman stumbled into the backyard followed by his wife.

James Anderson, a next-door neighbour, was just sitting down to dinner when he heard a scream, followed by a shot. He ran outside in time to see Forman and his wife coming down his garden path. He later testified that he heard Forman cry: "Mr. Anderson, Mr. Anderson, I'm shot! Schooley has shot me twice; I'm dying. For God's sake take me in." After making Forman as comfortable as possible, Anderson went for Dr. Helmcken and reported the incident to the police.

Officers Beecher, Clark and McEansom soon arrived and attempted to enter Foreman's house. Meanwhile, Schooley had locked both front and back doors, leaving a light burning in the dining-room and one in the bedroom usually occupied by himself and his wife. The Victoria *Colonist* picks up the story:

"The officers, after calling him to come out and getting only a curse in reply, burst in the front door and dashed into the hall. At the end of the hall is a glass door opening into the dining-room, and just as the officers opened this, Schooley stepped forward and fired one shot with a revolver, driving the policemen back into the street. He then came to the front door, pistol in hand, muttered a few curses and went inside again, shutting the front door. Meanwhile Inspector Bowden and Superintendent Sullivan arrived and concerted means for securing the assassin."

Several special constables were sworn in and the police, armed with revolvers and rifles, surrounded the house. However, although Schooley could be heard moving about frequently, it was not deemed advisable to force an entrance until about 11 o'clock. At that time, continued the *Colonist*, William H. Key "raised one of the kitchen windows and entered the apartment. He then opened the door and admitted Inspector Bowden and policeman Clark. The three groped their way in the dark to Schooley's bedroom, the door of which Mr. Kay found closed and Schooley lying against it. He pushed open the door and seized the wretch just as he was raising and had cocked a pistol to fire, and pinioned him. After this gallant exploit the Police entered the room and handcuffed Schooley, who seemed to be much under the influence of drink, and carried him (he refused to walk) to the barracks, where he now is. At Schooley's side were a demijohn of portwine, a six-shooter, a derringer, and a bowie-knife, and as Mr. Kay entered the room he stepped upon the revolver and it went off, doing no damage however."

Schooley was eventually tried and later in the year was hanged for the murder of Henry Forman, who died in Mr. Anderson's house at 11:40 A.M. on the morning after he was shot.

The second tragedy was just as dramatic. On November 4, 1875, the *Pacific*, a sidewheel steamer of 900 tons, was in Victoria Harbour taking on passengers for a scheduled run to San Francisco. Two of the men making the fateful voyage were Sewell Moody and Frank Garesche, two of the Eureka mine owners. Around 8 P.M. that night the *Pacific* was 40 miles south of Cape Flattery when she was accidentally rammed by the *Orpheus*. Fatally wounded, the *Orpheus* settled fast, breaking in two just before she disappeared beneath the waves. Although the precise number of persons will never be known, the official estimate was 275. There were only two survivors, Neil Henley and Henry Jelly. Mine owners Sewell Moody and Frank Garesche had gone to a watery grave.

From that time on, the history of the silver mines has been sporadic, to say the least. William Teague, reporting for the *B.C. Minister of Mines* in 1875, stated: "Operations at the Eureka and Van Bremer silver mines have been at a stand still, although, from each of these mines, specimens have been assayed with such results as would justify a vigourous development of the mines."

Around 1875-76, the mines were shut down. According to Loughnan, "owing to disagreement among the shareholders as to ownership and management, further development was abandoned." C.E. Cairnes, in *Memoir 139*, published in 1924, added that "litigation" was involved.

(Above) The road leading up Silver Peak Mountain. Note the rusty mine equipment.
(Below) The interior of cabin on Silver Peak Mountain. Both photographs were taken by Mike Fenske in August, 1993.

(Above) This Silver Peak Mountain mine adit can be seen from the cabin.
(Below) Core sample racks on top of Silver Peak Mountain. The Fraser River and Valley is visible in the background.

In any event, there is no evidence to indicate that a lack of valuable ore was in any way responsible for the closure.

The next reference to the mines appeared in the *B.C. Minister of Mines* for 1890, when William Dodd reported: "The Eureka and Victoria Companies have not been carrying on work of late years, but I am pleased to say the company (composed of wealthy Victorians) has been remodelled in the past year, with a view to resuming vigorous operations next season."

This does not appear to have happened, however, because the next information about the mines does not appear until 1902, when Dodd, once again writing in the *B.C. Minister of Mines,* reported: "The excellent trail to the cabin and workings is still in good condition. No work, or even prospecting for new ground, has been done for many years." A similar statement was made in 1903.

That might well have been the last time we ever heard of the mines on Silver Peak Mountain, had it not been for Arthur Williamson. Having heard rumours about a "lost" silver mine near Hope, for several years, Williamson decided to investigate in the summer of 1920. So as not to arouse suspicion, he took along a rifle and pretended to be hunting goat, just as the original discoverer had done 50 years earlier.

Leaving the railway two miles below Hope, Williamson followed a good road for about two miles. Then, after some difficulty, he located the old overgrown trail that led up to the mines. After climbing steadily for about a mile, the trail passed through what had been "an old camping place and horse corral. Then just at the edge of the timber line, an old cabin was found built by real axe men, in the construction of which wooden pins had been used in order to save nails. Old fashioned tools and utensils lay scattered about."

Inside the cabin Williamson saw "an old cast iron stove, and a huge open fireplace." In one corner lay the remains of an old assay outfit; in another, Williamson found an old 90-pound English anvil and a lot of hand steel. (Loughnan claims the anvil bore the inscription "Patented by Peter Wright, 1812," but there is mention of this in Williamson's article.) After digging around the cabin, a pile of ore samples was found.

The following morning Williamson decided to search for the old workings. After some difficulty, an old trail was found which led down along the face of a steep cliff. Following this trail to a narrow ravine, Williamson found the ruins of an old blacksmith shop.

"Surmising that the ravine was caused by the erosion of the vein," he wrote, "and that consequently the tunnel would be found under the snow, I walked over to what appeared to be the hanging wall where I found a crevasse between the rock and the hard snow, and climbing down into it I could see that I was right as to the location of the tunnel.

"Just ahead a few feet I could see the timbers of the first set, and working my way towards them I found that I just had room to crawl in between the cap and the muck that had accumulated in the mouth of the tunnel. . .As the air was good I continued on to the face 190 feet where I found a wooden car with iron wheels as good as new, and a few tools as though the miners had just gone off shift; also candles (tallow dips) were found stuck in the lagging ready for use. The track was also in good order, no rot being observed in the wood.

"The tunnel had apparently been driven in on the ore following a soft gouge, no crosscutting had been done, but after seeing their tools, and knowing that they only had black powder with which to blast, I could not blame them for not crosscutting."

After removing some ore from the face, Williamson left the tunnel and continued his exploration. About 500 yards from the entrance, "in the face of an overhanging cliff, I found the stone walls of an old camp." Williamson concluded that this was the remains of the old Victoria House, on the Victoria claim. "Built on a ledge 15 feet wide, the over-hanging cliff acting as a roof, the stone walls acting as the ends, the front apparently had ben constructed of logs from which was a sheer drop of 300 feet into a small lake, from which they got their water."

Loughnan claims Williamson also found a pair of crutches that had once belonged to S.P. Moody's father-in-law, and a patent medicine bottle marked "Langley Bros., Victoria," but Williamson makes no mention of these items in his article. Loughnan also claims that Williamson found the names of eight former employees, Stocker, McMaster, McMillan, Ned Atkins, Van Bremer, French, McEvoy and Murphy, carved on wooden timbers in the Van Bremer tunnel. Again, Williamson makes no mention of such a find.

Although Williamson published the story of his discovery in the Vancouver *Daily Province* on December 16, 1921, there was no new information to report until 1924. In the B.C. *Minister of Mines* report for that year, A.W. Davis, quoting from information obviously provided by Williamson, wrote that the Eureka-Victoria property had only been reopened within the last two years. Davis had visited the site in mid-May, but "owing to altitude of about 5,000 feet above sea-level, deep snow covered the mouth of the tunnel visited and it was now necessary to dig several feet through the snow to gain access to it." This tunnel, one of the original workings, was "200 feet long" when seen by Davis. Davis then went on to add:

"A report received recently from the management of this property states that since my visit this tunnel has been advanced (to) 450 feet with satisfactory results, and that a contract has been let to drive a 175-foot crosscut tunnel to cut the vein at a depth of 300 feet below this level. It is also stated that 150 feet of snow-sheds have been built and a permanent camp constructed for the crew."

In closing his report, Davis noted that five tons of ore had been shipped to Swansea in 1924 "which sampled 268 oz. in silver, with val-

ues in lead, copper and antimony as well."

Once again, however, the mines of Silver Peak Mountain were abandoned. But there appears to be no available information to explain why this latest venture, spearheaded by Williamson, failed. By all indications and assay reports, the mines were reported to be rich in silver. So, if it was not a lack or valuable ores, was it excessive transportation costs of lack of capital that hindered the latest attempt? We may never know.

However, the possibility that a rich silver mine lay forgotten on this mountain peak was so intriguing that I decided to investigate for myself before making the general facts known. On August 4, 1990, accompanied by my 14-year-old-son and 10-year-old daughter, I decided to try to reach the old mine site. Today, of course, you can drive right to the base of the mountain. From there I had hoped to learn the proper trail from a B.C. Government Forestry Map. Unfortunately, the map for Chilliwack Forest District was out of print. As a result, we took the wrong trail, one that led up Sowerby Creek. After climbing steadily for about an hour or so, I realized the trail we were on was not the correct one, so we returned to the car. There was another trail possibility waiting to be explored, but my son and daughter had had enough "exploring" for one day, and I had to agree that our failed first attempt had drained much of my enthusiasm.

As we left, my son and I planned to return at a later time, equipped this time for a possible overnight stay. Until then, I decided to sit on the story. It was only in August, 1992, that I was finally able to obtain a copy of the Chilliwack Forestry Map for the area, and a quick examination indicated that no trails existed to the mountaintop. Since this meant the planned trip would be far more arduous and time-consuming than I was prepared to tackle at this time, I decided to publish the story in *Canadian West* magazine so other adventurers could take up the challenge. One of my subscribers, Mike Fenske of Delta, B.C., decided to do just that. As I was putting the finishing touches on this chapter for the book, I received a letter and a number of photographs.

"As I enjoy both hiking and B.C. history," Fenske wrote, "I decided that this would be an interesting place to visit." Fenske purchased a National Topographical Map (92H Hope, 1:50,000) and a Provincial Topographical Map (92H SW Chilliwack, 1:100,000), both of which showed roads up the mountain. In mid-July Fenske visited Victoria where he purchased an aerial photograph of the mountain from Maps-BC. Looking over the photograph, the roads were definitely visible.

"Plans were made and a friend (Jim Cartlidge) and I hiked up the mountain on a day trip on August 4. None of the road was drivable so we had to hike all the way. I figure the distance was six or seven km up with an elevation gain of almost 5,000 feet. It was easy hiking at first, but after an hour or so the 'road' became so overgrown with small alder trees it was hard to see your feet at times. A small slide had occurred about two km from the start which was tricky to cross. After hiking for about two-and-a-half hours we came across a cabin which was in excellent condition and provided a nice break from the black flies. The cabin was of fairly recent vintage (maybe 15 years old) and must have been built when the road was still driveable: nobody could have packed the couch and mattresses up the trail. Inside we found a log book with interesting reading and a sign that stated that the cabin was maintained by the A.D. Rundle Outdoors Club... The most recent entry in the log book was for July of 1993.

"After resting for 30 minutes or so we decided to continue. Another hour found us above the alders and looking at a few racks of old core samples. A little further found us at an old mine adit. We had made it! Some pieces of pipe were lying around and down the hill a short way was a half buried piece of equipment with rubber tires. Obviously this was of more recent vintage than 1924 and the cabin was probably built for this more recent operation. A cool breeze was coming out of the mine as well as flowing water and a set of rails. About eight inches of water was standing in the mine so I walked in on one of the rails about 50 feet. It started to get dark and my little flashlight wasn't enough. Although it was about 2:30 by this time and we had a long hike back, we decided to continue until 3:30. We hiked up the road a little farther and came to a clearing at the top which is about where the 1924 camp should have been according to the map in your magazine.[1] Not much was visible, except a fallen down wall of an old building.

"Following the road, it was easily driveable at this point, we continued downhill and crossed an old slide, probably the one indicated on your map. Another mine adit was visible up the slide, but we didn't have time to climb up to it. Carrying on a short ways we finally came to Blue Lake. It was 3:35. We had left the truck at 10:45, so it took us almost five hours, including rest stops and exploring to reach the lake. We rested for 10 minutes and since it was getting cloudy and we had been hearing thunder for the last hour, we decided to head down. We stopped on the way back for a couple more pictures, a 20 minute rest at the cabin and a 10 minute rest at a creek crossing further down. We got back to the truck at 6:45, three hours after leaving Blue Lake for a total of eight hours of hiking."

Fenske concluded his letter by stating that he hoped to return one day when he would have more time to look around, possible staying overnight in the cabin, which would avoid the necessity of packing a tent up the mountain. Fenske's letter and photographs confirm that two mine adits are still open and accessible. Possibly he or someone will bring this story to a successful conclusion one day.   ❀

---

1 The map, which appeared in black & white in the magazine, is reproduced in full colour on page 22.

CHAPTER 3

BULLDOG KELLY'S
BURIED LOOT

In 1884 a whisky salesman was making his way south from Golden with two other men when the party was bushwhacked by a lone gunman. The holdup, during which one man was killed and another wounded, netted the gunman $4,500. Rumours still persist today that the outlaw buried the loot near Golden, British Columbia.

OUR strange tale of murder and lost treasure began on the cold and snowbound morning of November 27, 1884, as a party of three men made their way south through a rocky ravine 25 miles south of Golden, British Columbia.[1] "In the half-light of dawn, three horsemen picked their way, single file, through snowdrifts which covered the narrow, winding trail. Leading was a man named Manvel Drainard, followed by well-known Montana liquor salesman Robert McGregor Baird. Popularly known as Harold Baird, the American was returning to Missoula, Mont., with his seasons receipts for Eddy, Hammond & Co. It had been a good trip; in his bulging pocket and saddlebag was $4,500 in gold and currency.

"Bringing up the rear was his packer and guide, a half-breed named Harry."[2]

The three were proceeding southward at a casual pace. Suddenly, as they crossed a wider stretch in the trail, tragedy struck. "Baird was halfway across when, without warning, a shot punctured the stillness. The heavy ball caught him square in the chest, spinning him, lifeless, from the saddle. Taken completely by surprise, Drainard snapped a frightened look back, saw Baird pitch to the ground, then spurred his mount. Unarmed and

MANVEL DRAINARD

---

1 For the purpose of this investigation, two accounts of the murder-robbery will be examined. Cecil Clark served with the British Columbia Police for 35 years, rising to the rank of Deputy Commissioner. After his retirement in 1950 he started writing about his experiences and the experiences of other policemen. Clark appears to have started the rumour about the buried loot in his article "Fate Set Penalty for Killer of the Kootenay," which appeared in the Victoria *Daily Colonist* on October 11, 1959. The second major account was written by T.W. Paterson, an author of several books and numerous articles on B.C. history. His version, "Bulldog Kelly—Cold-Blooded Murderer," appeared in *Outlaws of the Canadian Frontier*, (Langley, 1974: Stagecoach Publishing, pp. 38-45).

2 T.W. Paterson, *op. cit.*

(Above) This painting, by artist Joe Adams, depicts Paterson's version of the confrontation between Harry the packer and murderer Bulldog Kelly. It shows Harry withdrawing his rifle and about to engage in a gunfight with the killer. Another version, by ex-B.C. Provincial Policeman Cecil Clark, claims Kelly was on horseback during the robbery.

totally unnerved, his only thought was to get beyond range. The terrified youth charged off down the trail, leaving hapless Harry with a corpse and a hidden killer.[3]

Glancing wildly about, Harry spotted the sniper just as he fired a second bullet that tore into the packer's hip.[4] "The concussion almost knocked him from the saddle but, regaining his balance, the courageous half-breed jerked his rifle from its scabbard, levered a shell into the breech and fired, all in the same motion."[5]

Harry's shot whistled harmlessly into the trees as the startled robber fired his third round, which also missed. "Before either could reload, Harry had closed with the stranger. The frightened horses collided, squealing, riders savagely jousting with empty rifles. His wound forgotten in the heat of battle, Harry leaped onto the murderer, both men

3 *Ibid.* Clark's version is slightly different. He wrote that as the three men "rounded a bend in the river-edged trail they were suddenly confronted by a mounted stranger — a stranger with a Colt .45 in his hand who peremptorily ordered the travellers to throw up their hands."

"Baird made a move for his gun, but was just a split second too late. A bullet from the outlaw's gun caught him in the chest, and with a groan he slid out of the saddle. Sprawling on the ground, Baird expired at his horse's feet."

4 T.W. Paterson's version. Clark contends the bullet hit the packer in the shoulder.

5 The painting accompanying this story was based on Paterson's version and was commissioned for the cover of his book.

(Above) Work crews laying the prairie section of the CPR for the movie "The National Dream."
(Right) A CPR class A3m 4-4-0 locomotive which was restored for the movie.

crashing heavily to the ground."[6]

"For several fast-moving minutes the two engaged in a clawing, gouging, foot and fist encounter, that saw the combatants locked in their struggle rolling over and over on the rocky trail, each trying desperately to gain an advantage. Finally the outlaw belted Harry into unconscious with a rock, and staggered over to Baird's horse rifled his saddlebag of $4,500 in cash and made off."[7]

"When Harry came to, he was alone. Easing himself to his feet, he surveyed the grim scene dizzily. It took several seconds before his reeling senses cleared enough for him to observe the killer's handiwork. Baird lay in the mud where he had fallen, almost naked. The highwayman had methodically slashed open his clothing, even removing boots and socks. Nearby, Baird's horse grazed quietly, freed of saddlebags. These too had been slashed apart and ransacked.

6 T.W. Paterson, op. cit. Clark wrote that after being shot in the shoulder, Harry "dismounted and using his horse for cover, rushed the outlaw on foot and not only wrested the pistol out of the highwayman's hand, but hauled him off his mount."
7 Cecil Clark, op. cit. Paterson states Harry simply lost consciousness from loss of blood and shock.

"But Harry was not thinking of the missing money. He had just enough strength to clamber into the saddle and knee the animal toward Kicking Horse, booming construction camp of the building Canadian Pacific Railway (CPR). It was nightfall when the battered guide arrived. He was almost unconscious, eyes and mouth swollen shut, teeth caked in dried blood. Somehow he managed to mumble details of Baird's murder. As someone ran for medical assistance, Harry mustered his last surge of will power to describe the killer, then passed out."[8]

Harry described the murderer as "about 30, tall and powerfully built, with reddish hair and a reddish moustache. He wore a black felt hat, dark overalls and a black sateen shirt."[9] According to Clark and Paterson, the description enabled the police to identify the murderer as "none other than Bulldog Kelly, a big, red-haired, loud-mouthed character from the States, who had been seen up and down the Kootenays for a year and had recently been seen in Golden."[10]

Soon a manhunt was underway for the killer as outraged railway construction workers eagerly volunteered to join the posse being formed by North West Mounted and Provincial Police officers. Fanning out from Golden and Kicking Horse, the posse combed every ravine, every creek bed, every goat track that might offer an escape to the murderer.

However, despite an intensive search, spurred on by a $1,000 reward offered by Eddy, Hammond & Co., and $250 added by the province, Kelly had vanished without a trace. It was a big, rugged country, and even Indian trackers had little success following the signs left at the murder scene. The single, solid clue they found was the murder weapon; Kelly had dropped or thrown the rifle into Kicking Horse River.[11]

The police, being tipped off that Kelly was in Golden, instituted a thorough search of the town and vicinity but failed to find a trace of the wanted man. Kootenay Gold Commissioner Vowell dispatched two more constables to assist the investigation at Kicking Horse.

A week or so later the search had slowed to a frustrating crawl. Scant clues were forthcoming, and it looked like Kelly had succeeded in escaping to the American side. Then, whether acting on a hunch or on some new information, one of the policemen decided to have the Winnipeg bound train searched. Firing off a telegram to a water stop ahead of the train, he asked the crew to check its passengers for Kelly, without, if possible, arousing his suspicions if he was aboard.

"Coincidentally, among the passengers were two qualified to act upon the request; none other than Col. A.G. Irvine and Col. McLeod of the NWMP. The telegram gave a brief outline of Baird's slaying and

---

8. T.W. Paterson, *op. cit.* Clark states Harry went to Golden to spread the alarm.
9 Cecil Clark, *op. cit.* Paterson's description has the outlaw at "about five feet eleven inches in height. . . blue eyes, mustache of a light color, turned up at the ends, reddish complexion, and chin whiskers apparently cut with scissors. . .dark suit, sack coat and Scotch cap with peak."
10 Cecil Clark, *op. cit.*
11 T.W. Paterson, *op. cit.* and Cecil Clark, *op. cit.*

(Above) Golden City, B.C., 1884, The building, centre
left, was called the CPR Hotel.
(Right) Const. John Kirkup, c1894.

Kelly's description. Colonels Irvine and McLeod
decided it was a good time to stretch their legs
and separated.

"Irvine spotted him first. Dressed in the
rough garb of a railway worker, the red-haired
suspect was watching the vast prairieland
sweep by his dust-streaked window. Irvine
strolled through the car, seemingly preoccupied
with his own thoughts, passed the stranger,
then paused at the end of the car. This was
Kelly, he was sure. Without glancing back, he
decided to arrest him then and there rather than wait for McLeod.

"When Irvine turned—the man was gone. The alarmed officer
strode to the door, jerked it open and stepped onto the platform. He
almost collided with Kelly, who was leaning against the railing. Just as
Irvine 'put out his hand to arrest him. . .' reported the Victoria *Daily
Colonist*, 'the man LEAPED FROM THE TRAIN, which was not running
at a very rapid rate. He was not injured, and the moment he regained his
feet he ran for dear life across the plains'."[12]

Months passed, without another clue as to Kelly's whereabouts,
although the police were certain he had returned to the United States.
Concentrating their search by circular, Canadian authorities gave his
description to law enforcement agencies as far south as Oregon, as far
east as Minnesota.

---

12 Paterson and Clark state essentially the same thing. However, there is no record of this incident in
A.G. Irvine's Annual Reports for 1884 and 1885. However, there is a different version of this event,
which will be revealed later.

The CPR tracks alongside the Kicking Horse River, Yoho National Park, July 1990.

Eight months after the murder of Baird, provincial constable Jack Kirkup of Revelstoke found Kelly. Working on special orders from Victoria, with permission of Minnesota authorities, Kirkup finally traced the wily suspect to Crookstone.[13] Once he had found Kelly, it was an easy matter to have him arrested by local marshals. Extradition, however, would be a different matter.

It seems that Kelly had influential friends in high places, and they created one roadblock after another. Despite the determined efforts of B.C.'s Dep. Att.-Gen. Paulus Irving, assisted by Const. W. McNeil, provincial authorities were stalled at every turn. It was seven long months before Canadian authorities were even able to bring Kelly before U.S. Commissioner Spencer in St. Paul. The Canadian effort was finally rewarded when Commissioner Spencer ordered Kelly extradited. But it would be a fleeting victory.

Undaunted by the decision, Kelly's lawyer, "Big Tom" Ryan, caught the next train to Washington, D.C. where he met with the Secretary of State Thomas F. Bayard! The strategy worked.

"Raged the Victoria *Colonist:* 'The refusal of Washington authorities to make the order for the extradition of Bulldog Kelly does certainly not indicate the existence of that reciprocal feeling which the province has always manifested in assisting the U.S. to bring fugitive criminals to justice.

"In no civilized country is the laxity of its laws so noticeable as in the U.S., where the law's delay too often end in their final evasion. Whether the prisoner Kelly is innocent or guilty, it is evident to all those who have read copies of the deposition of witnesses in the case that there is ample ground to warrant the order for the prisoner's extradition. The fine scrupulousness displayed in this instance by the American authorities would almost incline one to the belief that extradition on a charge of murder to B.C. meant the prisoner's subsequent conviction of the crime.

"The attitude of the province in these matters displays a striking contrast to that of its powerful neighbor. Our local governments have invariably proved themselves as indefatigable in detecting and arresting extraditable fugitives from the states as if the law had been outraged in our own country; thereby observing the true spirit of the treaty — to expedite the administration of justice apart from the consideration in which of the two countries that justice was contravened.

"The editorial concluded: ". . .It would be well for (U.S. authorities) to. . .recognize the rights belonging to Canada as a party to the existing treaty, and facilitate, not obstruct, a country whose only fault may be that in the administration of justice she is more tenacious in effort, a lesser respecter of persons, quicker to try, as slow to condemn, and swifter to

13 T.W. Paterson, *op. cit.* Clark says he was found in St. Paul. However, Sam Steele wrote that it was a Winnipeg policeman named Murray who found Kelly in the U.S. Also, according to *British Columbia Illustrated* (R.E. Gosnell, 1906), Kirkup was policing the CPR at Savona from August, 1884, until May, 1885, at which point he was transferred to Revelstoke. Thus Kirkup's involvement in this case will require further scrutiny.

execute than any other constitutional government on the American continent."[14]

"Finally Washington was moved to action; but not of the kind B.C. was hoping for. Instead, convinced by Ryan's gilt arguments, the extradition order was quashed. Stunned but not beaten, Mr. Irving's squad immediately countered with another affidavit, this time that of Manvel Drainard.

"Once again, the Canadians went before Commissioner Spencer, and once again he heard Ryan's tirades and writs of *habeas corpus*. And once again the weary commissioner accepted B.C.'s case, committing Kelly for extradition. Jubilant with victory at last, Irving and his witnesses headed home, leaving the constables to follow with the prisoner.

"This time it had been Ryan's turn to express amazement. He and his two colleagues had constructed what he considered a perfect battery of nine defence witnesses—'four to prove an alibi and five to impeach the veracity of the witnesses for the Crown.

"'These witnesses for the defense had been, in November, 1884, engaged on the construction of the CPR, and in Kootenay district it would have been easy to show the reputations they had earned for themselves, but at St. Paul it was not open for the prosecution to do so. All the prosecution could do was to show by the inconsistencies in their evidence that their story was not worthy of credence. This was undertaken by the prosecution, and, as the commissioner has committed the prisoner, we may presume it was attended with success.'

"The *Colonist* ended with a last complaint: 'The proceedings were conducted with a licence that would not be tolerated in a magistrate's court in this country—the prisoner enjoying a cigar and conversing with his many sympathizers'."[15]

But, justice for the murder of Baird would again be denied, as Ryan returned from Washington with a final decision from President Grover Cleveland himself. It was a long story of backroom politics. Apparently Ryan had told the president of Kelly's past good work for the Minnesota Democratic Party. Not to mention the fact he was Irish, although the Irish might not have been so loyal to Kelly had they known he was born Edward Loughlin—in Illinois.

Kelly, now a free man, said: "It is good news. . .I have no idea as to whether the Canadian authorities will carry the matter further, but I don't propose to stand any more of it. It is a persecution of the worst kind, and ought to stop right here. I've been in confinement eight months for nothing, as the decision shows. The stories of my being well supplied with money are not true. I had $10 when I was arrested, and with the exception of $100 paid Mr. Steenerson for me, that is all the lawyers have received for my case. If the Canadian authorities push it further, I'll bring

14 T.W. Paterson, *op. cit.* Paterson's version of the extradition proceedings is more detailed than Clark.
15 Quoted by T.W. Paterson, *op. cit.* The date of the newspaper article was not provided.

up stronger evidence than shown yet."[16]

Bulldog Kelly drifted back into anonymity until April, 1890, when fate accomplished what Canadian justice could not. Kelly was employed as a brakeman on the Northern Pacific Railway running into Helena, Montana. On this fateful day Kelly was supposed to have told some members of the train crew that he was making his final trip. He was going to B.C. where, he hinted, he had some money cached. A few minutes later, as the train slowed for the yards, Kelly was observed running along the top of a string of boxcars, when suddenly he stumbled and fell between two of them. Both legs had been severed below the knees, and although Kelly was rushed to a hospital, he died a short time later.[17]

INVESTIGATING THE FACTS

One of the difficulties with this particular story is the lack of documentation in the newspapers of the day. To compound this problem, Kelly was never brought to trial, so the details of the case are extremely difficult to pinpoint. However, with the limited records I could discover, I will try to reconstruct the murder and robbery.

This incident occurred during CPR construction through the Rockies. In the spring of 1884, Sam Steele of the NWMP was instructed to select 25 volunteers to police the railway's right-of-way. Three men were stationed at Laggan (Lake Louise), two at Third Siding (Field), eight, plus Steele, at Golden, four at First Crossing, two at Beaver Creek, two at the Summit of the Selkirks, and four at Second Crossing (Revelstoke).[18]

The belt over which the NWMP had jurisdiction was initially only 20 miles wide, 10 miles on either side of the railway. This area had been proclaimed by the Canadian government under the Act for the Preservation of Peace on Public Works, which meant the sale of intoxicating liquors was prohibited.[19] Unfortunately, light fines—$40 for the first or second offence[20]—was not much of a deterrent. Compounding the problem was the narrow belt of law enforcement. Dispensers of spirits simply erected their crude establishments outside the 10-mile limit, and thirsty railway workers did not hesitate to travel the distance each payday. After Steele's recommendation that the belt be widened to 20 miles on either side of the right-of-way was passed, the situation improved somewhat. But the sale of illegal liquor still posed a serious problem.

To satisfy the demand for booze, bootleggers had it brought in from Montana by pack train to meeting places at the Hog Ranch and on Baird's Creek.[21] Harold Baird was apparently one of the rum-runners involved in transporting illegal whisky within the railway belt, and he

16 Quoted by T.W. Paterson, op. cit. Source not provided.
17 T.W. Paterson, op. cit. and Cecil Clark, op. cit.
18 1885 Annual Report of the NWMP, p. 16.
19 S.B. Steele, *Forty Years In Canada*, (New York; Dodd, Mead & Co., 1915), p. 186.
20 *Ibid*, p. 186.
21 Thomas King, *The Story of Golden*, p. 5. King moved to Golden in 1899 and later compiled a brief history of the area.

A view of the CPR's station and community of Glacier, B.C., c1913. Located on the CPR right-of-way a few miles south of Roger's Pass, it may have been the route Kelly took after his murder-robbery. Somewhere near here, two members of the NWMP spent the night in Kelly's camp, unaware that he was the cold-blooded murderer they were seeking.

had just been paid for his pack train of Montana liquor.[22] A man named Johnston[23] ran the roadside inn known as the Hog Ranch[24] and it was he who reported the murder-robbery, which occurred three miles south of his establishment, to Steele.[25]

The only newspaper being published in the general area at the time was the Calgary *Herald*, and it published only a brief news item about the murder-robbery based on a letter it received dated December 4. The letter stated that the three men were riding in a single file when ". . .all of a sudden, a shot was fired from someone in the bush. The second man (Harold Baird) dropped dead, shot through the heart: the first (Manvel Drainard) put spurs to his horse and escaped; while the third (Harry), finding his horse not fast enough for him, jumped off and ran back

22 *Ibid.*

23 S.B. Steele, *op. cit.*, p. 183.

24 During the days of whisky smuggling, one of the establishments serviced was in this log building. One day a preacher stopped there during his travels and saw that the "members of the household and the horse wranglers of the pack train were lying around in a drunken stupor. The man of God remarked that they looked like hogs, and the title 'Hog-Ranch' was given to this place for many years. A nearby creek is still marked on modern maps as Hog-ranch Creek, but the settlement is now known as Parsons, after an early property owner." *Kinbasket Country: The Story of Golden and the Columbia Valley*, Golden & District Historical Society, 1972, p. 23.

25 S.B. Steele, *op. cit.*, p. 193.

towards Johnston's ranch. While doing so he received a shot in the leg, but succeeded in reaching the ranch, having returned from a side cut. Several men then proceeded to the scene of the murder, and found the body of the murdered man in the middle of the road, with his horse a short distance away. It seems that the murderer, finding no money on the body, had given chase to the horse, caught it, cut open the pack, and relieved it of $4,500, and then made good his escape."[26]

Where Paterson and Clark got their information about a gun battle and a hand-to-hand fight between Kelly and Harry is unknown. According to this account, both Manvel and Harry fled the area immediately after Baird was killed, with Harry being wounded in the leg as he did so.

The only police report I could find of the event is unofficial and was written 30 years after the event. According to Steele, after being informed of the murder-robbery, he sent two men in pursuit. Meanwhile, Johnston, assuming the murderer was heading south, notified the Indians in that area to be on the lookout.

The two Mounties sent by Steele "went to the place and searched for tracks, and found three 45.75 Winchester cartridges behind an uprooted tree from which the murderer had fired his fatal shot. They also tracked him back to where he had spent the night at a fire in the woods, and from there to where he stood early in the morning on the hill above the hotel (Hog Ranch), watching the little party make their preparations to start, whence he was tracked back to the pine-root where he posted himself to do the shooting. Another strike from there resulted in finding where he had run after the pack-horse, caught it and cut open the pack, evidence that he was no packer. The tracks were followed through the ford at Golden, and in it a new Winchester rifle was found; three shells had been fired and five were in the magazine. The constables reported that Drainard had stated that the man was unknown to him, but wore a beard, was tall and had a stoop. I sent them on, caused every camp to be visited, wired to the Winnipeg police and to every point east and south, to the Attorney-General of British Columbia and to our headquarters.

"The two constables went as far as the Second Crossing of the Columbia, now Revelstoke, and to rest their horses slept at a camp in the Selkirks, in a tent with a man named Bull Dog Kelly, who was going in the same direction. He was the murderer, but in no way, except as regards height, did Drainard's description tally with his. Kelly disappeared at the Columbia, and for a time we were completely baffled."[27]

There are some obvious inconsistencies in the accounts of Paterson and Clark with what Steele reported. The most glaring of these is the fact that the police did not know who the murderer was because Drainard, through apparent fear for his life, provided them with a false description. As a result, instead of the NWMP solving the case in a few days, they

---

26 Calgary *Herald*, December 17, 1884.
27 S.B. Steele, *op. cit.*, pp. 193-194.

unwittingly allowed Kelly to slip through their fingers.

The next opportunity to capture Kelly, on the train, is also described by Steele. On July 19, 1885, he was in Calgary where the citizens gave him a banquet and a diamond ring for his work during the Riel Rebellion. Shortly afterwards, Steele went to Winnipeg for 10 days. A few days later, the young constable who was with Steele rushed up to him. The constable, who was returning from the Winnipeg races, told Steele that he had seen "the ruffian 'Bull Dog Kelly' on the train coming from the races." Kelly had asked the constable if he had a warrant for his arrest. The constable "had replied that he knew of none, and had scarcely spoken when Kelly jumped off the train near the station and disappeared.

"On hearing this it struck me that Kelly was the man who had murdered Mr. Baird the year before, and I reported this to Murray, of the Winnipeg Police, who had been informed by me of the murder and the large rewards offered for the arrest of the murderer, and he came to the same conclusion as myself, that Kelly was the man. Accompanied by Sergeant McRae, until two years ago (1913) chief of the force, Murray went in pursuit of Kelly. Taking the train to Crookston, Dakota, they found him in one of the hotels. Stealing cautiously up to his bedroom they hurled themselves against the door, bursting it open and securing their man. Had they undertaken the arrest in any other way there would have been some shooting! They then lodged their prisoner in gaol in Crookston to await an investigation, and I hurried back to the Rocky Mountains to have the case worked up. When I arrived there I found that Drainard, who had known all the time but was afraid to speak, was now ready to swear that 'Bull Dog Kelly' had fired the fatal shot. What an amount of trouble we should have been saved had he spoken out at the time!

"The evidence was damning and conclusive but, although the commissioner reported in favour of extradition, the authorities in Washington would not sign the papers, and Kelly was released, but was again arrested in Minneapolis and brought before another commissioner, with the same result. The Attorney-General, or his deputy, from Victoria, B.C., was there watching the case for Canada, but as the proceedings had already cost many thousands of dollars it was not deemed wise to do any more. The murdered man was an honourable American citizen; the murderer was an American. We had done our duty according to our traditions of justice, and there was nothing to be done but abandon the case. Kelly died a violent death the following year. His right name was McNaughton, and during the trials he was encouraged by the fact that the desperado who had inspired the crime was present with a large amount of money supplied by the criminal class in Chicago and the members of a secret organization noted for its hatred of everything British."[28]

SUMMARY AND CONCLUSION

As I have already stated, there are numerous discrepancies between the

28 *Ibid*, pp. 232-233.

accounts of Paterson and Clark, and the documentation I was able to compile. Having said that, however, I must also point out that these discrepancies are details in historical accuracy which do not enhance or nullify the possibility of buried outlaw loot. I will now examine the treasure angle more closely.

The first time Clark mentions the treasure is following the encounter between Kelly and Baird. Whether or not fisticuffs took place between Kelly and Baird is highly debatable, at best. However, for the sake of argument, lets assume that it did. Clark wrote: "In the half hour that elapsed before the packer was able to regain his feet and his senses and finally mount his horse, the holdup man had somewhere along the trail buried the currency under a rock before he continued his flight."

That single sentence, completely unsubstantiated by anyone or anything, is the only implication of buried treasure. On what basis does Clark make this profound assumption? This solitary reference to buried loot, upon which the entire "lost treasure" aspect of the story revolves, is totally without foundation. There simply is no documentation I have uncovered to justify such a hypothesis, and Clark does not refer to any. This assertion, in my opinion, was simply an attempt by Clark to romanticize his article by tossing in the very remote possibility that Kelly had buried the $4,500.

I simply do not believe that Kelly would have planned and carried out such a cold-blooded murder-robbery just to bury the money and walk away. The only purpose for doing so would be if he was afraid of being caught with it in his possession. However, with or without the money, if Kelly had been apprehended and identified, he would have gone to the gallows. To suggest that Kelly concealed his stolen loot, and planned to return for it later, is poppycock. I just do not buy it. First, the robbery occurred in winter, and the possibility of relocating the same spot in summer time would be doubtful, at best. Second, the NWMP who investigated the murder traced Kelly's movements through the immediate area by his footprints in the snow. Had he in fact buried the money, his tracks would have led the police directly to it. Finally, if Kelly was afraid of being captured with the money, the sensible thing for him to do was conceal it near his camp each night. That way, if Kelly was visited by police, which he in fact was, the loot would be nowhere in sight.

There is only one reference to Kelly's financial well-being, and that occurred eight months after the murder when he was seen on the train coming from the Winnipeg races. What would a man with no money be doing at the races? The amount stolen in the robbery, $4,500, would not last forever. Gambling, drinking and carousing in camps throughout the west would soon eat away at the proceeds of his ill-gotten deed. For me, the story of Bulldog Kelly is a fascinating episode of frontier life along the CPR right-of-way, nothing more, nothing less. ❦

Chapter 4
The Gold Boulder Of Kootenay Lake

In 1892, four men supposedly found a solid boulder of gold which they estimated, at that time, to be worth over $860,000. According to the story told by the man who made the discovery, while trying to transport the treasure to Nelson, the 2,366-pound boulder crashed through the floor-boards of the boat and sank in 400 feet of water.

COME AGAIN

IN GRAY CREEK

HOME OF THE GOLD BOULDER

IN 1988-89, while preparing the book *West Kootenay: The Pioneer Years*, I had occasion to research every frontier newspaper published in the West Kootenay region. In so doing, I discovered two fascinating lost treasure stories. The first, "The Lost Rocker Mine," appears later in this book. The second is the story I am about to relate.

Prior to reading this story, which appeared in a Nelson newspaper over 100 years ago, I had never heard about Kootenay Lake's gold boulder. The following account, told by one of the actual participants, is quoted essentially as it appeared.

ORIGINAL LEGEND

"Two years ago this month,[1] the writer was camped at the head of Crawford's Bay, the east end of Kootenay Lake. This bay, five miles in length, is on the east side of the peninsula which puts out into the lake with Pilot Bay and Cape Horn on its extreme southwestern corner, and a short, low, narrow projecting ledge of slate rock on the southeastern corner called Cockle's Cape, named in honor of two young Englishmen who had the foresight and energy to pre-empt a ranch at the head of Crawford's Bay and improve it when this whole country was little more than a vast wilderness. Between Pilot Bay and the main lake, on the narrow neck of land back of Cape Horn, the Kootenay Reduction Company were at that time actively engaged erecting their vast buildings, which can now be seen every day by travellers on the passing steamers.

"I had several times explored this peninsula, searching for minerals in veins, but had never been rewarded by discover-

(Main photo) Looking down Crawford Bay from the wharf at Gray Creek.
(Inset) Sign publicizing the gold boulder at Gray Creek.

1 April, 1892.

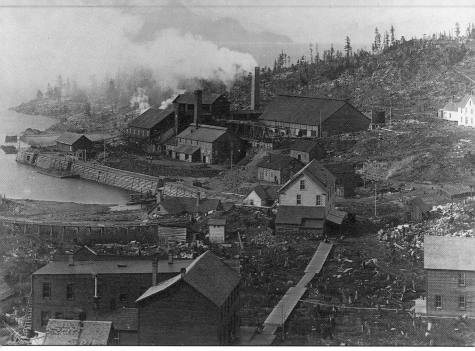

According to Kemp, the Kootenay Mining and Smelting Company was just getting start-
ed when the gold boulder was found. The Pilot Bay operation is shown here c1896.

ing anything that would pay. I had, however, found numerous boulders
of galena, carrying pyrites of copper. These boulders were plentifully
scattered over the ground and ranged in weight from a few ounces up to
probably 100 tons. The existence of this lead and copper on the ground
described is well known to scores of residents, and I may make mention
of the fact so as to what my companions and self afterwards discovered
in the same locality.

"The fall before, the manager of the works being erected at Pilot Bay,
with other supplies for the winter, had secured a number of beef cattle.
Two of these bovine had strayed away and were presumed to be about
some of the small natural meadows which were to be found on the
peninsula. At the time of which I write a reward had been offered for the
return of the cattle or their carcases, which would be quite a grub stake
for my companions and myself, as our prospecting ventures had not
realized our fond hopes and we were getting toward that point where
we would resemble many United States banks during the panic—pay-
ment suspended. Lured by the reward for the cattle, we decided to give
up hunting for mineral wealth and endeavor to locate the beef bonanza.

"Now a brief description of my comrades in the thrilling experience
which follows. There were four of us. I will not give full names, and
because space is valuable will shorten them. There was "Jim, Bill, Joe"
and the author. Jim and Bill were brothers, Joe was a prospector who had
drifted to us and we had kindly taken him in. Jim was the mathematician

of the crowd, and reduced everything to figures. He could glance at a steamboat on the lake, calculate her tonnage in an instant, and tell how much money the owners had in the bank. He would size up a pile of sawdust near a sawmill and instantly tell how many feet of lumber had been cut and how many fish the dust would kill were it to be turned loose on the lake. Once I ventured to give him a problem as follows: 'If an elephant can chase a raw oyster up a sour apple tree, how many shoestrings will it take to fatten a lamp post?' He started to figure, then looked at me with an angry scowl and said, 'You's better go and soak your head.'

"Bill's mind ran toward chemistry. He always had a laboratory, drug store, and general reduction works about when prospecting. He could take a piece of rock, manipulate it and tell to a nicety how much gold, silver, lead, anti-fat, and parasites of poverty it contained. He could carve a gnat or buffalo with equal ease, and set them up, preserving contour and expression so thoroughly that their own mother would not know they were dead.

"Joe was a rollicking, good-natured fellow, who could play seven-up and had the faculty to tell yarns in such a comical manner that we were always in splendid humor. He has gone back to Oregon, and may better success crown his efforts than while with us is our best wishes. The fourth member of the party was the writer, whose extreme modesty and thorough regard for truth precludes giving any description of himself or alluding to his accomplishments.

"Bright and early in the morning we left our camp to strike the trail and trace up the vein of beef, which if found and delivered at the smelting works would bring us about the princely sum of $15 each. Little did we anticipate that we would return to camp that night individually worth nearly one-quarter of a million dollars in gold.

"We took two boats; Jim and Bill in one, while Joe and myself occupied the other. We pulled down the bay toward the main lake about two and a-half miles, landed, and prepared for our cattle hunt. Besides some provisions, a small axe and a gun, which we carried with us, I had taken my small pole-pick along to break any rock encountered so as to ascertain if it was mineral bearing. We struck out and thoroughly explored the eastern side of the peninsula, examining the small meadows for the stock or their tracks, which would lead us to them should they be hidden from view in a thicket. All our efforts were futile. We saw neither beeves nor tracks, and about 4 o'clock in the afternoon the four of us came out on Cockle Cape as before described. Weary with day's exertion we all sat down far out toward the point of the cape where we were surrounded on three sides by water and were watching the heaving bosom of old Kootenay while speculating on our ill success. I, prospector-like, was striking at a boulder covered with soil and debris from the surrounding trees. Finally, I noticed that the point of my pick adhered to the object. Calling

The cliff in the centre of this photograph is suspected as being the one from which the gold nugget was being lowered when the rope broke and the boulder crashed through the boat and into the lake. (Left inset) Tom Lymbery, of Gray Creek. (Right Inset) the logo of the 1964 treasure hunters.

the attention of my companions to this fact, we scraped the covering away and were surprised to find the boulder, or as much as was exposed, was a yellow metal. This naturally excited us somewhat, so we began digging around it, one of the boys made an improvised shovel out of a piece of cedar. With a broom made from fir branches we shortly had the lump of metal and the bed-rock around it (it rested on solid foundation) swept clean. We used our axe as a chisel and the pole-pick as a hammer and before long had quite a sample chipped from all the sides exposed. These we examined in the sunlight and in the shade, as prospectors do when in doubt with an auriferous specimen, and we were unanimous in the opinion that the boulder at our feet was a huge lump of virgin gold. I shall not attempt to describe our feelings or actions at this particular point. Jim was the first to arrive at a practical basis. Taking from his pocket a two-foot rule he began measuring the nugget. Then he said: 'Boys, it averages 27 inches long, 14 inches deep, and 12 inches wide, and there is not a particle of quartz about it.'

"When we had all realized the immensity of the find which the blind goddess of fortune had thrown in our path, we began to devise ways and means to transport and dispose of it so as to reap the benefit. It was now getting late in the evening, so we carefully covered up our treasure and with light hearts returned to our boats and rowed to camp.

"Occasionally a feeling of doubt would enter our minds that perhaps the lump was not the metal we took it for, but, Bill, who was a chemist, dispelled all such thoughts when he had thoroughly tested it by boiling our samples in nitric acid and comparing on a touch-stone our gold with some which G.W. Hale had brought down from Duncan River. Jim, who had been figuring during this time now announced his results. 'Boys,' he said, "I have measured that nugget carefully, 27x14x12 equals 4,536 cubic inches. A cubic inch of gold weighs 10.55 ounces, therefore there are 47,854.8 ounces in that chunk.' Then Bill says, 'and the gold is identical in grade with this which old man Hale brought from the Duncan river.' 'Then,' replies Jim, after making a few rapid strokes with his pencil, 'our day's work brings us $861,386.40, or $215,346.10 each, as Hale's gold is worth fully $18 an ounce.'

"Naturally, we poor soldiers of fortune, so suddenly and unexpectedly raised from dire poverty to affluence, began to speculate on what we would do with our money. Bill, among other things, was going to construct a yacht which would outdistance anything that every floated. Joe, who had prospected from Old Mexico to Alaska, intends to gather up all the worn-out burros over the mining country where he had travelled and put them on a ranch in Oregon, which he would purchase for that purpose. I was just beginning to tell how I would endow a sanitarium for worn-out prospectors, when practical Jim suggested that we had better decide on some method to turn our wealth into cash before we laid plans to spend it. Various means were suggested, and we were about to adopt the plan of cutting it up with chisels where it lay when Bill aired a new idea which had just struck him.

"'Now boys,' he says, 'that man Seever is liable to be here next week to work on some claims for a Spokane syndicate. If he should come he would naturally want a share in our discovery. If we let him know anything about it he will make us trouble. Now we must get our gold here to camp, conceal it until Seever gets through and leaves, then we can cut it up, melt and run it into bars at the company assay at Pilot Bay, when the banks in Nelson will do the rest.' 'Now listen to me,' interposed Jim. 'This lump weighs nearly two tons, it isn't safe to leave it where it is, and we have got to get it here to camp where we can watch it. Now in a few weeks the lake will raise about 18 feet vertically. Tomorrow we will put in a false bottom of two-inch plank in our largest boat, load the nugget into it, bring it here, then cover it over so no one will know what it is, as the beach rises we will keep drawing the boat up the beach; then when the water receded the boat with its precious load will be high and dry on shore. By that time Seever will be gone and we can arrange to dispose of our metal.' We all coincided with Jim in his plans and all determined that the grasping Seever should have no share in our lucky find. Being tired out by the day's exertions and subsequent excitement, we each sought our bunks for repose.

"When I awoke next morning Bill was getting breakfast. He informed me that Jim and Joe had the false bottom in the large boat. After finishing our meal we provided ourselves with two crowbars and a cant-hook from the ranch and some inch rope, the heaviest to be had; placing these, together with an axe, pick and shovel, in our boats, we were soon speeding toward the cape. Arriving there the large boat was moored close up against the rocks and while Jim, Joe and I were cleaning the soil off bedrock to make a solid track on which to roll our boulder, Bill was cutting two skids on which to slide the heavy weight down into the boat. The frail vessel lay, by measurement, 14 feet vertical below the top of the ledge; for this reason the skids were to be used. We made a sling of part of our rope, rolled the nugget onto it, then brought one end of the sling through the other and fastened the single rope to the bight. A convenient tree for snubbing was at hand, around which the rope was wound. The skids were in place, Jim took his stand at the tree to do the snubbing; Bill, Joe, and I, by exerting all our strength, turned the nugget over so it rested on the upper part of the skids; the rope became taut, stretched to its utmost tension; the skids spread apart. Crash! We peered over the rocky ledge, our boat was kindling wood and 400 feet of the blue waters of Kootenay lake hid our beloved nugget from view. The rope had parted.

"Randall H. Kemp
"Kaslo, April 17, 1892."[2]

2 This article appeared in the Nelson *Tribune* on April 23, 1892.

INVESTIGATING THE FACTS

The first things I usually check when trying to validate or discredit a particular treasure story are the participants. In this instance there were four principal characters, although the full name of only one, the storyteller Randall H. Kemp, is revealed. Essentially, I seek three things when researching the characters. First, can I verify their existence. If I can, I then want to know if they were known to be in the area at the time the story took place and if they were credible.

With Kemp I was fortunate enough to find two quick references. The first, which appeared in the Ainsworth newspaper under the heading "Kaslo Notes," read: "Mr. Kemp, proprietor of the mineral springs near here, made his first shipment of mineral water Thursday to Nelson and Pilot Bay. He says that the demand already exceeds his present limited means of supply."[3]

The second reference was even more impressive. In 1893, the B.C. *Minister of Mines* published an 11-page detailed report on the Slocan mining district, covering history, location, geology, mines, prospects, etc. Preceding this report was the following paragraph:

"The following comprehensive and accurate description of the Slocan country is mostly taken from a report written by that well-known and practical miner, Randall H. Kemp, for the Nelson *Tribune*, and is considered by all acquainted with the country, as an accurate and reliable report of what, in the near future, promises to be the greatest mineral producing district in the world."[4]

These two items not only verified the existence of the storyteller, but established Kemp as an "accurate and reliable" authority on mining in the region. Unfortunately, I was not nearly as successful with regards to his three companions, primarily because Kemp did not divulge their last names. Kemp's reason for not doing so, "because space is valuable," is ridiculous, since it would only have added four words to the story. Instead, Kemp gave paragraphs of frivolous background information about them, most of which cast doubts on the veracity of the story itself.

Nevertheless, I did make an attempt to identify his partners. Joe, could be anyone, so I did not even bother with him. But the fact that Jim and Bill were brothers offered a slight clue. Occasionally, the newspapers published a list of voters for the area. I scanned these looking for brothers named Jim and Bill. I was able to track down only one possible combination, J.F. Phillips and W.C. Phillips.[5] Unfortunately, I was not able to verify if the initials "J" and "W" stood for James and William; and even if they had, there is no guarantee they were Kemp's partners.

Kemp says the discovery was made at Cape Cockle, which was named after two Englishmen. Although they were not directly involved

3 Ainsworth Hot Springs *News*, July 13, 1892.
4 B.C. *Minister of Mines*, 1893, p. 1052.
5 Nelson *Miner*, October 24, 1891.

in the treasure story, they apparently had a ranch at the head of Crawford Bay. This part of the story was rather easy to verify through a couple of items I found in the Ainsworth newspaper. The first read: "The Cockle brothers, boat builders of Crawford's bay, have turned out another specimen of their handicraft, this time a double racing skiff with sliding seats. . . ."[6]

The second item was an advertisement: "RANCH TO LEASE. The owners of 320 acres, including hay meadow, wish to let the same, under an improvement lease for a number of years. Good dwelling house and buildings. Particulars may be had from Green Bros., Ainsworth, or from Cockle Bros., Crawford Bay."[7]

Thus the Cockle brothers were indeed real and in the area at the time the story took place.

Kemp gave the treasure story some historical background when he referred to Pilot Bay, and stated that they were searching for cattle that had escaped from the manager at Pilot Bay. Once again, history backs up this part of the story.

"The Kootenay Mining & Smelting Company is leaving nothing to chance in the erection of its reduction plant at Pilot Bay. The site has been carefully surveyed and accurate soundings made for the wharves. The plans for the buildings were not made until the ground was first carefully examined by a representative of the firm furnishing the machinery. The bricks needed will be made near the site, the brick machines being already on the ground."[8]

By the early summer of 1892, the works were progressing nicely:

"The first thing one sees at Pilot Bay is the wharf (it is all wharf at present) the next is Dr. Hendryx. If the wharf is everything the doctor is everywhere, busy and cheerful, on the best of terms with himself, his men, and the world in general. "We have over 400 feet of wharfage now, and there will be more when it is completed," said the doctor. But if it is all wharf now, it will not be so long. Men are busy excavating a site for a concentrator which, along with the smelter site, will be levelled down to the

6 Ainsworth *Hot Springs News*, October 3, 1891.
7 Ainsworth *Hot Springs News*, April 6, 1892.
8 Nelson *Miner*, November 28, 1891.

(Above) Gray Creek 1964-65. The float used by Card and Babich is clearly seen in the water. Behind the bushes on the far right-hand edge is part of their float house. (Opposite page) These two chimneys are all that remain today of Pilot Bay.

wharf and the intervening space made solid with the rock and dirt taken out. The smelter or concentrator will lie immediately to the north of the wharf. Dr. Hendryx does not expect that either will be completed this summer. Further to the north on the top of a small rise is the boarding house which will be completed and occupied within a week or two. It is a model of its kind. It contains a good sitting room for the men, while it is fitted up with bath-rooms and other conveniences which do not always come the way of the workmen in western towns.

"South of the smelter site lies the town of Pilot Bay represented at present by a restaurant in a tent and the unfinished store of the Galena Trading Company. During the last six weeks about 50 acres of the townsite have been cleared and the timber converted into cordwood. The company mean to grade streets and lay down sidewalks at once. . . ."[9]

SUMMARY AND CONCLUSION

In July, 1993, I made a trip to Kootenay Lake to obtain photographs for this story and any additional information I could find. One of the places I visited was the Gray Creek Store, operated by Tom Lymbery. Lymbery knew the general story of the gold nugget and told me that he was aware of at least one group who had tried to recover it.

In late February, 1964, two men named Card and Babich stopped at the Gray Creek Store to rent a boat. When one of the men asked what the fishing was like at Cape Cockle, Lymbery knew they were after the gold boulder. As he wrote: "no one refers to Cape Horn as Cape Cogle[10] unless they have been reading the story of Gray Creek's gold boulder."[11]

After swearing Lymbery to secrecy, the two men informed him that they were indeed after the long lost treasure and they intended to stake a claim across the bay from his wharf.

"A few weeks later one of the men, Stephen Babich, returned with an older aluminum boat with 25 h.p. Evinrude on a home made trailer. He arranged to park his vehicle and trailer in Gray Creek Auto Camp— his home was in Castlegar. He spent a lot of days out in his boat and in early May he came in pushing a log float that he had designed—a section cut into the float just fitted his boat so he could push it as one unit—boat and float. A smart move if you have ever tried towing a float or even logs with an outboard—the tow has a mind of its own and is uncontrollable at times.

"I envied his project—beachcombing the logs, crosspieces and framing. Beachcombing on the lake has always been more interesting than fishing, you never know what you might find. Babich's float had a heavy duty arch frame of 6x6 timbers and underneath this was a trap door covering a cut out in the logs. With 2x4s and plywood he framed and roofed a cabin on his float—with a door but no windows.

---

9 Ainsworth *Hot Springs News*, May 4, 1892.
10 Although Lymbery spelled it "Cogle" in his article, the correct spelling is "Cockle."
11 *Mainstreet*, June 1993, p. 13. *Mainstreet* is a monthly magazine-type newspaper serving the east shore communities of Kootenay Lake.

"Like any prospector he was close lipped, except that he needed investment in his project, so he was able to assure that his scheme would be most profitable."[12]

Lymbery was surprised when the treasure hunters set up an underwater camera with a submersible that could be controlled from the surface. The two men later told Lymbery that they had recovered a sample from the boulder, although it was not revealed how this was accomplished in 200 feet of water. Up to this point the men had kept costs down by improvising. Having located the nugget, however, they needed divers, and divers cost money, which they apparently did not have.

"They kept their claim in good standing. The float had been anchored at the claim site the first year but it was too exposed to the wind, so they brought it over to our side of the bay. I told them where there was an old B.C. Forest Service anchor chain so this became a safe spot. A couple of years passed and they let the big float strand at high water. Babich made a smaller float and did have a skin diving crew out, but 200 feet is just too deep.

"By 1972, Card had left the partnership and Babich approached me to see if I could take some of his equipment off his hands, so I ended up buying his boat and motor and the float house. We eventually got an offer for the latter—it fitted the long haired dreams of a houseboat with no taxes! It changed hands many times and each owner made changes to the structure which was tied at Picnic Bay."[13]

While these men obviously believed in the lost boulder story, Lymbery never told me if he did, and I forgot to ask. Personally, I am not convinced that the gold boulder ever existed. I am leaning toward the distinct possibility that the story was a cleverly crafted tale told purely for entertainment purposes. It is too incredible for me to believe that four men, who knew exactly where a gold boulder worth over $800,000 had sank, never made any attempt whatsoever to try to recover it. WOW, now that really stretches the imagination!

Also, where did the mysterious 2,366-pound nugget come from. A boulder of this size, of almost pure gold, simply does not grow out of the ground, and I doubt very much that it fell out of someone's pocket. If there were rich gold quartz veins or placer deposits in the area, that might suggest a source for the gold boulder. There is none. In fact, the area was noted for silver, not gold. The Bluebell mine, in particular, was rich in silver.

Our fascination with lost treasure will ensure that this tale will survive for another 100 years or more. Unfortunately, unless someone can suggest a plausible explanation as to how the nugget came to be where it was supposedly found, it will remain an interesting piece of West Kootenay folklore, and it should not be elevated to anything more than that. ❀

12 *Ibid.*
13 *Ibid.*

CHAPTER 5

OLD MAN GREEN'S MISSING HOARD

It was just over 100 years ago that the white sandy beach of tranquil Savary Island, near Lund, B.C., was bloodied by a shocking double murder. Yet rumours that one of the murder victims, old man Green, buried his wealth on the island, persist to this day.

IF a pirate wanted to conceal his ill-gotten loot on an island along British Columbia's inside passage, Savary Island would make the ideal choice. It would be very easy to visualize a pirate vessel anchored just off the crescent-shaped shore of white sandy beach on this picturesque island just southwest of Lund. Certainly Capt. George Vancouver had been impressed by the island when he landed "on a delightful plain with a fine, smooth beach" in July, 1793, and named it Savary.

But Savary Island was off the beaten track, and nearly a century passed before it attracted its first permanent resident. From Virginia City, Nevada, John Green first arrived in B.C. in 1871 and took up farming in the Nanoose District of Vancouver Island. After several years, Green sold out for a small profit and moved to nearby Englishman River, where he purchased a share in the farm of John Hirst.[1] In 1888, Green sold his share in this farm and moved to Savary Island, where, on October 24 of that year, he purchased lot #1372, 160 acres, for $160. Green was obviously fascinated with the island, for on August 2, 1891 he purchased another 317 acres, followed by the purchase of an additional 316 acres three weeks later. By the time Green added another 151 acres through preemption on October 3, 1893, he owned 80 percent of the island.

By this time "Old Man" Green, as he was affectionately known, was nearly crippled with arthritis and was only able to move about with the assistance of two canes. Nevertheless, he had managed to clear a spot from the forest near the beach on the northeast tip of the island where he erected a log cabin and store. Green earned his living by purchasing furs from passing Indians, trading in return canned goods, fishing gear, clothing, hardware, tobacco, powder and shot. His most popular item was

The hotel and harbour at Lund, just north of Powell River, in 1989.
(Inset) A map of the Savary Island area.

---

1 From single page biography on file at Powell River Museum, researcher unknown.

SAVARY ISLAND

Hernando Island

LUND →

Savary Island

This area enlarged below.

Oyster River

Harwood Island

Powell River

POWELL LAKE

Cape Lazo

COMOX

Courtenay

Cumberland

TEXADA ISLAN

N

Government Wharf

Site of Old Man Green's Store

(Above) These were the first permanent buildings erected on Savary Island. The log building in the foreground was Green's trading post. It was connected by a breezeway to a 15x25-foot cabin, seen on the left, that served as living quarters. It was in this latter building that the murders occurred.
(Below) John Green's property on Savary Island at the time of the murder-robbery. Both photos were exhibits presented during the trial.

fresh meat, obtained from his flock of 300 sheep, as well as cattle, pigs and chickens.

Green had the reputation of being an honest trader and his business flourished, hence he was able to continually add to his holding of Savary Island property. But Green was also rumoured to be "flush with cash," their being no banks nearer than Nanaimo or Vancouver. Each time he visited Lund for supplies, he unabashedly displayed a thick roll of bills.

Because of his arthritis, Green had advertised for a man to work for him. Several men had applied and some had been employed for short periods of time, but all had either left of their own accord because of the isolation, or were fired by Green for being lazy. One day an old friend, Thomas Taylor, arrived on the island. Green offered his old friend a share in the business if he would stay, and the two entered into a successful, but short, partnership.

Just before noon on October 30, 1893, Norman Smith and Dick Lewis, returning to Nanaimo from a trip to Hernando Island, decided to visit Green's small trading post. When they landed on the beach they were met by four Indians, a man and three women, who told them that there was no one was in the store. As Smith and Lewis started to make their way up the beach, Albert Hanson arrived on the scene. The three men then continued up to the store. Finding that it was locked, the threesome went to the adjoining cabin and knocked on the door. When there was no answer, Hanson opened the door and entered, followed by Smith and Lewis. Neither of the three men were prepared for the gruesome scene which lay before them. Green's spartan one-room quarters were even messier than usual. Besides the crude furniture, household items and empty liquor bottles scattered about, the ransacked cabin also contained two bodies. At the subsequent trial of the murderer, which was covered by the Vancouver *Daily World*, Smith described the grizzly scene. Green's body lay near the entrance to the cabin with his head against the wall and his shoulder against the door. Green appeared to have been getting dressed when the murder occurred. This was suggested by the fact that his trousers were at his ankles and he only had one sock on. "There was blood on Green's body from his breast to his knees. There was blood on Green's shirt and breast. There was blood on a chair and on the door knob."[2]

Taylor's fully-clothed body, continued Smith, was lying on its face. Bullets had been fired through pictures, the clock, a lamp and through the walls. A loaded shotgun lay beside each body, one half-cocked, the other was full cock. The first impression the three men had was that Green and Taylor had argued over something and fought a deadly duel. This was suggested by the weapons found beside the bodies and from 13 bullet holes found throughout the cabin. However, it did not take long to dispel this theory since none of the bullet holes, including those which killed Green and Taylor, had been made by a shotgun.

Seven spent 44-calibre shells found lying on the floor instead suggested that the two men had been killed by a third, as yet unknown, assailant. Hanson, a former employee of Green, knew that he generally slept with a cash box under his pillow. It was now missing and was later discovered in a trunk, empty, except for $10 in gold that had been overlooked in one compartment. Green's pocketbook was also found, and it too was empty.

While Smith and Lewis remained at the murder scene, Hanson went

2 Testimony of Norman Smith, as reported by Vancouver *Daily World*, July 17, 1894.

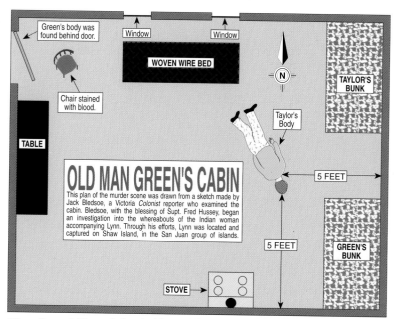

Green's body was found behind door.

Window

Window

WOVEN WIRE BED

N

TAYLOR'S BUNK

Chair stained with blood.

Taylor's Body

TABLE

5 FEET

OLD MAN GREEN'S CABIN

This plan of the murder scene was drawn from a sketch made by Jack Bledsoe, a Victoria *Colonist* reporter who examined the cabin. Bledsoe, with the blessing of Supt. Fred Hussey, began an investigation into the whereabouts of the Indian woman accompanying Lynn. Through his efforts, Lynn was located and captured on Shaw Island, in the San Juan group of islands.

5 FEET

GREEN'S BUNK

STOVE →

(Opposite page) The sandy beach of Savary Island showing the government wharf. (Below) A row of bungalows stretch along the northern shoreline of Savary Island. The building on the far left is situated approximately where John Green erected his store and cabin.

over to Lund to spread the alarm. Word of the tragedy was then relayed to Mike Manson, Justice of the Peace of Cortes Island, who, accompanied by Const. Walter B. Anderson and Dr. A.H. Thomas from Comox, steamed northward in his little launch *Stella*. Meanwhile, Charles Thulin, owner of the Malespina Hotel at Lund, sent four men to Savary Island to examine the scene and remain with the bodies until the police arrived three days later.

When Manson, Anderson and Thomas viewed the scene, their first impression was the same as Smith, Lewis and Hanson. Green sat behind the door, a shotgun at his side, a gaping hole in his chest. Taylor, his assistant and friend, lay face down in the middle of the room, also atop a shotgun. Bullet holes were everywhere.

But it did not take long for Manson and Anderson to realize what had really happened. Both men had been murdered by a third party, probably with robbery as the motive. The murderer then made a very clumsy attempt to make it appear that Green and Taylor had killed each other during an argument. But the murderer had been so inept, if it had not been for the seriousness of the crime, it would have been comical.

For a start, although both men lay on shotguns, an examination proved that neither weapon had not been fired in months. Furthermore, both victims had been killed by a rifle, probably a .44 Winchester. The killer had also neglected to retrieve the spent rifle cartridges. Green was known to own two Winchesters, both of which were missing. In addition to this, when Taylor's body was turned over, he still clutched a pipe in his left hand, something he was not apt to do during a deadly battle. Further investigation revealed that the bullet holes in the walls had all been fired from the centre of the room.

Dr. Thomas concluded that the men had been murdered on October 26 or 27. The time of death was established at 10 minutes past 10. This was decided by a clock, smashed by a bullet, which had stopped at that time. On November 4, Thomas performed a post mortem examination of the bodies, and at the trial revealed his findings. The bullet that killed Green had been fired from above the body and "had ploughed through the lungs, passed through the liver, broke the eighth rib on the right side, and finally brought up against the spinal column. There was much internal and little external bleeding. His stomach was healthy and contained partly digested food."[3] Green had died instantly.

The wound that had killed Taylor had also come from a point higher than the body. "It broke the rib just under the collar bone. It tore the main arteries and the jugular vein. The bullet went downwards, struck the spinal column and turned back and lodged in the right kidney. There was part of the shirt in the wound. The stomach was healthy, and contained partly digested food and more fluid than there was in Green's stomach."

3 Testimony of Dr. A.H. Thomas, as reported by Vancouver *Daily World*, July 19, 1894.

After completing his examination of the cabin, Constable Anderson moved to the store. The door was still locked, as the loggers had reported, but a side window had been smashed. A muddy footprint on the sill confirmed that this was how the killer had gained entry. In the grass Anderson found several grains of bird-shot and a plug of tobacco, which the murderer must have dropped while leaving. Upon entering the store, Anderson saw that it too had been looted, although he had no way to determine what had been stolen.

Having completed his examination of the murder scene, Constable Anderson crossed over to the Malespina Hotel. There, hotel owner Charlie Thulin stated that he had last seen Green and Taylor on October 24. He had seen them twice that day. The first time was when he went over to Savary to deliver a bag of seeds Green had ordered. Green paid him $12 for the seeds and $35 on his account. Besides Green and Taylor, another man named Hughie Lynn was there. Later that day Green and Lynn visited the hotel where they had a couple of drinks, paid for by Green. After a couple of hours they returned to Savary. In the evening, between six and seven, Lynn returned to Lund with an order from Green for six bottles of whisky. Thulin gave him the six bottles and also filled another bottle Lynn had with him, making seven in all. Before leaving, Lynn told Thulin that he was going to stay with Green all winter, and that his "Klootchman" was going to do the cooking.[4]

After questioning Albert Hanson, Anderson learned more about Lynn. Hanson had been employed by Green for about three weeks, from the last week of September until October 16. In early October, Lynn showed up at the island in a skiff with an Indian squaw and her young son, but left a few days later. A week or so after he quit, Hanson was fishing outside of Lund when he was approached by Lynn, who asked if he was still working for Green. When Hanson said no, Lynn indicated that he was going to visit Green, hopefully to get a job. Hanson did not return to Savary until October 30, when he discovered the bodies with Smith and Lewis.[5]

There was now a growing suspicion that Lynn was responsible for the cold-blooded murders, and from all the evidence gathered to date, Anderson was able to reconstruct what had probably happened. When Lynn, the Indian woman and the boy first visited Savary Island in early October, it was probably for no other reason than to purchase tobacco or supplies. Once there, however, Lynn's perspective began to change. Perhaps Green's well-stocked store was too tempting a target. After all, it was on an isolated island, owned by a feeble 67-year-old man. Or perhaps it was the rumours that Green kept money stashed on the premises. Lynn may have decided to rob Green then and there, but hesitated from doing so because Green's employee, Hanson, was also on the island. In

4 Testimony of Charles Thulin, as reported by Vancouver *Daily World*, July 19, 1894.
5 Testimony of Albert Hansen, as reported by Vancouver *Daily World*, July 19, 1894.

any event, Lynn left the island a few days later and headed north. When he returned about two weeks later he learned that Hanson was no longer working for Green. With the old man now alone on the island, Lynn began to plan his robbery.

Unfortunately for Lynn, Green's old friend Taylor returned before the robbery could be carried out, so Lynn had to delay his plans yet again. It is not known if Lynn was able to gain employment from Green, but he nevertheless camped on the island and began to frequent the cabin and store. Two days before the murders the three men went on a drinking spree together.

On the morning of the murders the three men awoke and ate breakfast. This was indicated from the three sets of dirty dishes and the partially digested food in the stomachs of Green and Taylor. After breakfast, the three men probably finished off the remaining whisky. Green sat in the chair beside the door, Taylor sat on the side of his bed, smoking a pipe. At some point, just as Green bent over to pull on his trousers, Lynn decided to carry out his scheme. Standing between the two men, he shot Green first, the bullet causing instantaneous death. Wheeling around just as the astonished Taylor started to stand, he shot him with the second bullet. Taylor probably staggered a step or two before collapsing face down on the floor, still clutching his pipe.

In an attempt to make it appear that the two men had killed each other in a quarrel, Lynn then sprayed the room with bullets. He then placed shotguns beside each body. Unfortunately, in his frenzied, drunken state, he did not think too clearly. Thus he overlooked the fact that neither shotgun had been fired in months, neglected to realize that his victims were killed by a rifle, and carelessly forgot to remove seven rifle cartridges from the cabin floor.

As an intensive investigation was conducted into the whereabouts of Lynn, it was learned that his father had been one of the original Royal Engineers. Hugh was born on the ship that brought them to B.C. in 1858. After the Royal Engineers disbanded in 1863, the Lynn's settled on the north shore of Burrard Inlet. Today, Lynn Canyon and Lynn Creek are named after them.[6]

Although the Lynn's were a hard-working, respected family, young Hugh had been troublesome since boyhood. "Now at 35," wrote Cecil Clark, "he was a beachcomber and squaw man, travelling the gulf in nomadic style, doing a little trapping, usually to be found in some Indian rancherie. Wherever he stopped in his wilderness wanderings, the sail from the skiff formed a tent fly, and the trio subsisted on mowitch, clams and grouse until he had a few mink or otter skins to sell."[7]

As the days dragged into weeks, no leads were forthcoming on the present whereabouts of Lynn, his squaw or the young boy. It was as if

6 Cecil Clark, "A Little Boy Told of Savary Island Slaying," article in the Victoria *Colonist*, April 4, 1965.
7 *Ibid.*

they had disappeared from the face of the earth. Then, about a month after the murders, a new piece of evidence emerged, Lynn's skiff. Actually, the boat had been found and picked up by Hugh Keller, a resident of Oyster River, on October 30, the same days the bodies had been discovered. However, a month was to pass before anyone connected the skiff with the murders and Constable Anderson was ordered to investigate. An examination of the boat revealed some shot in the bottom, the same as had been dropped by the murdered when he exited the store. But of Lynn himself, there was not a sign.

As the months rolled by the police became increasingly frustrated by the lack of information. F.S. Hussey, Superintendent of the B.C. Provincial Police, said at the subsequent trial that a warrant was issued for the arrest of Lynn, and every effort possible was made "to affect his arrest." Hussey had sent a description of the trio to cities around Puget Sound, in the event the murderer had gone to the United States. Finally, after months of frustration, the investigation began to yield results.

It was learned from an Indian woman at Bella Coola that the Indian woman accompanying Lynn was named Jenny. She had once been married to an Italian named Boketo at Port Townsend, who had since died. The boy was named Louis. Further investigation at Port Townsend revealed that Boketo had left Jenny a lot and cabin on Shaw Island, in the San Juan group, near Friday Harbour. Following the leads, Hussey located the cabin. It was empty, but Hussey learned that a white man resembling Lynn had been seen there recently. On April 9, 1894, Hussey returned to the island accompanied by an American sheriff. As they approached the cabin they noticed smoke coming from the chimney. Hussey walked up to the front door and knocked. When a man's voice from inside invited them in, the policemen entered.

Once inside, Hussey immediately recognized the man to be Lynn, but remained calm and asked for a glass of water. Lynn offered the men a glass of wine. Hussey then asked the man his name. "He replied 'Gallagher,' but immediately afterward said, 'No, it's Newton'."[8]

While this brief conversation was taking place, Lynn became suspicious and started to edge his way to where a Winchester was hanging on the wall. However, when Hussey stepped between Lynn and the rifle, the fugitive bolted for the door. This time there would be no escape, Lynn being promptly placed in irons and deposited into the San Juan county jail.

Lynn waived extradition and was subsequently returned to Victoria where he was placed in jail pending his trial in Vancouver, which began on July 17, 1894. The Hon. A.N. Richards and Dep. Att.-Gen. Smith appeared for the prosecution, while E.P. Davis represented Lynn. By this time the police had accumulated a great deal of evidence against Lynn, although it was almost all circumstantial. The only two witness to the

8 Testimony of F.S. Hussey, Vancouver *Daily World*, July 19, 1894.

murder were Jenny and Louis Boketo. Seven-year-old Louis testified that after Lynn robbed Green, he broke the window and crawled into the store. After a long time, he emerged with some skins, clothing, shot and other items, and placed them in the boat. The prisoner also "had lots of guns in the boat."

Upon cross-examination, however, Louis testified that he had seen both Green and Taylor shoot. Since it was a known fact that their weapons had not been fired, Justice Drake considered the boy's evidence too contradictory, and disallowed it being presented to the jury.

Jenny had not seen the actual murders either, but she nevertheless provided the Crown with some very incriminating testimony. She described how Lynn came down to the beach with the stolen goods, how the two stolen rifles were thrown overboard, and how Lynn traded his .44 Winchester, the suspected murder weapon, to an elderly recluse. Some furs stolen from Green's store were traced with Jenny's assistance to the purchaser, H.S. Maybee, who was on hand to testify. The police also found the incriminating bag of shot at Lynn's Cape Lazo campsite with the help of Jenny. As the parade of witnesses continued, the actions of Lynn after the murders began to emerge.

After killing Green and Taylor, and stealing the money from Green's wallet and cash box, Lynn entered the store by breaking a window. After ransacking the store of some furs, shot and other items, he loaded the skiff and the trio set off for Cape Lazo, near Comox. Along the way Lynn threw Green's two Winchesters and some stolen items overboard. The second night after reaching their destination, the skiff got loose. Lynn claimed it was carried away by the tide, while the police maintained he set it free intentionally as he did not want to be seen with it. In any event, Lynn then purchased a canoe for $40, and after burying some of the items he had stolen from Green's store, particularly the shot, by which his movements had been traced from the store to the skiff, he headed south.

After leaving the Comox area, they went to Waldron Island, and then to Port Townsend, returning afterwards to the island. In January, 1894, Lynn visited the trading post of H.S. Maybee on nearby Orcas Island. Maybee testified that he gave Lynn goods in exchange for bear, otter and deer skins, which the prisoner had claimed he had obtained on the mainland. Maybee paid Lynn $2 for the bear skin and $1 for the otter, then sold them for $14 and $3.50 respectively. Under cross-examination, Maybee admitted it was the most profit he had ever made on a fur deal. Circumstantial evidence was also provided by George H. Perego, a pensioner, who testified that on April 6, 1894, Lynn traded him a .44 Winchester for an old Harper's Ferry rifle.[9]

On the final day of the trial, Lynn tried to convince the jury that he had acted in self-defence. Green and Taylor had quarrelled, and Green

9 Testimony of H.S. Maybee, Vancouver *Daily World*, July 19, 1894.

A rear view of Green's trading post, on the left, and his cabin at the time of the murder.

shot and killed Taylor, then fired twice at him, but missed. It was only after he had killed Green in self-defence that Lynn decided to rob the premises.

However, all the evidence presented by the Crown totally rejected this theory. According to Dr. Thomas, Green had probably been killed first. Also, Taylor was smoking when killed, something he was unlikely to do during a gun battle. Similarly, Green was only partially dressed, and it was inconceivable that a man who was a virtual cripple without his canes, with his trousers at his ankles, would cross the room to shoot Taylor.

It took the jury less than three hours to determine the fate of Hugh Lynn. He was found guilty of murder, but the jury recommended mercy. Justice Drake then asked the prisoner if he had anything to say why the sentence of the court should not be passed upon him. Lynn hesitated a moment, and "cast down his eyes. His lips twitched once or twice, and then he straightened up, and in a firm voice said: 'Nothing'."

Justice Drake then passed sentence: "Hugh Lynn, after a long and careful trial you have been found guilty of the wilful murder of John Green. I urge you to spend whatever time is left you in interceding with the throne on high for that mercy which you did not show to those two unfortunate men. It is my duty to pass the sentence of law upon you, which is that you be taken from the place where you now are to the place from whence you came and there be hanged by the neck until you are dead. And may God have mercy on your soul."[10]

Thus ended the capture and trial of Lynn for the murder of Green and Taylor. But what about the treasure?

It has often been stated that Green had "a thick wad of bills" esti-

10 Vancouver *Daily World*, July 21, 1894.

mated at between $300 and $500 at various times. However, since no one has ever provided an accurate count, the amount may have been much less. Unquestionably, however, there were times when Green did have a large amount of money, since he had purchased a total of 944 acres on Savary Island at $1 an acre. The pertinent question then, is how much money did Green have at the time of his death?

On October 3, 1893, just three weeks before his murder, Green had purchased 151 acres on Savary Island. If Green had possessed excess funds at that time, it is not unreasonable to assume he would had purchased more of the island, of which he now owned 80 percent. On October 24, two days before his death, Green paid Charlie Thulin $35 "on his account." Again, if Green had substantial funds available, why did he not pay off his account in full?

There is no record of how much money was actually stolen by Lynn. However, I would venture a guess that it was probably between $100 to $200, maybe less. We do know that Lynn emptied Green's wallet and cash box, except for $10 in gold which was missed. Of this, Lynn is known to have spent $40 for a canoe. But six months rolled by between the time of the murders and Lynn's capture, and it would not be difficult to imagine that the murderer, who in addition to himself, had a woman and child to feed, had spent all the money.

But, if Savary Island is not a "treasure island" in the monetary sense, with its warm waters and sandy beaches, it is a "treasured isle" to vacationers. Today there is a row of bungalows just off the beach beside the wharf, not far from where Old Man Green once operated his store. With no electricity, except for gas generators, and connected to Lund by water taxi, the island is a place to relax and dream. Small wonder then, that the legend of John Green's missing hoard has persisted for so long. After all, the lure of lost treasure gives this scenic island a mystique all its own. ❀

CHAPTER 6

ATLIN'S LOST ROCKER MINE

Did the story of a rich placer creek serve as the catalyst for the discovery of the Atlin goldfields? This is only one aspect of an intriguing lost treasure that is revealed here for the first time in nearly a century.

M OST lost mine stories are a combination of myth, rumour and legend, and it is often extremely difficult to uncover a shred of documented evidence to support its existence. In that respect, the Lost Rocker Mine, near Atlin, British Columbia, is different. The story of its discovery, how it was lost, and the details of a subsequent search for it, were all documented in at least one B.C. newspaper.

In 1988-89, while researching through pioneer newspapers, I came across an intriguing lost treasure story which was totally unknown to me. To my knowledge, except for the newspaper it first appeared in, this is the first time the details of this account have ever been published. It is certainly the first time the lost placer has been scrutinized for veracity.[1]

ORIGINAL LEGEND

"Several years ago an Indian came into Juneau, very much exhausted by privation and hardships and by the disturbed state of his mind, induced by brooding over a crime he had committed, and for which he gave himself up to the authorities there. His story, which fired the ambition and lust for gold in all who heard it, was one which is sometimes encountered between the yellow covers of a dime novel, but seldom indeed in actual life. He stated that far back among the mountains beyond Long Lake he had discovered a claim of such wealth that in three days he had taken out of it gold to the amount of $20,000. He and his squaw were working diligently at the claim when one day a white man visited their camp and ingratiated himself into their friendship. With the paleface the redskin shared the story of his discovery, and the two men set to work to further explore its richness. All went well till the Indian conceived a distrust of his squaw and of her relations with the paleface guests, and one morning, returning from his claim, the white man having feigned sickness, he found his worst fears confirmed and the unfaithfulness of his

---

1 I first presented this story in the Winter 1993 issue of *Canadian West* magazine,

A view of Juneau, Alaska, from the harbour, in 1894. The year after this photograph was taken, according to the legend, an Indian came to town revealing his story of murder and a rich placer mine.

squaw demonstrated before his eyes. In a rage he seized his rifle, and, first killing the woman, he dispatched her paramour with a rifle ball. Overcome by the enormity of his crime, and unable to bear his secret, he packed up his gold, and, tramping through to Juneau, told his tale to the authorities, at the same time exhibiting bags of yellow dust as a proof of at least part of his story. The aggravation to which the man had been subjected was considered sufficient to condone his crime, and he was allowed to escape unpunished. He rapidly pined away, however, and after describing as accurately as possible the location of the mine, he passed away.

"It was a rough plan made from the Indian's description of the spot that Colonel Hughes and Mr. Jones set out from Atlin lake last summer to see if they could not discover the rocker which had been deserted when the Indian's happy home had been wrecked by the ingratitude of his guest. Between three and four hundred men, they knew, had preceded them in search of the same locality, but in a country of such extent they knew that the late explorers enjoyed almost equal chance with the pioneers. The location of the mine, according to the Indian's story, was close against a glacier, at the foot of an extinct volcano, and the route to it lay along Surprise and Long lakes. The travelers set out in a canoe, and some distance up Surprise they found four others bent on the same errand. Reaching the head of Surprise they portaged to Long lake, and passed up its entire length, about 70 miles. The directions of the discoverer were that after reaching the foot of Long lake they were to paddle along its base, passing the mouths of six creeks. Upon reaching the seventh they were to ascend it, and by following it they would find the lost rocker and the deserted mine.

"After a laborious journey along the foot of the lake the mouth of the seventh creek was at last gained, and the explorers pushed the nose of their canoe against its waters. Buckbrush grew thickly on the banks and interlaced their arms across the stream, and for three days and a half the little party toiled against the current, the task being rendered doubly difficult by reason of inturning branches. At the expiration of that time they came to where the creek forks, one branch leading off to the left and the other to the right, inclining toward Surprise lake. Some hesitation was felt as to which stream should be followed, but the fact that provisions were running short and that the right branch bore them nearer to their base of supplies decided the question. This branch was followed some distance until the travelers saw looming before them the glacier and the volcano, with its smoke enveloped crown.

"Here the party spent three days in prospecting. Col. Hughes and Mr. Jones climbed the precipitous sides of the volcano, notwithstanding the protestations of their comrades,[2] who insisted that it was still active. Upon reaching the mouth of the crater they found that it was extinct, and that the topography of the country corresponded closely with the description given by the Indian. Thus reassured, they prosecuted the search for three days, but without finding any benches of extraordinary richness, and through the failure of supplies they were forced to abandon it.

"Mr. Jones, who is now at Victoria with one of his partners, W.D. Kinsloe, is, however, by no means satisfied that the lost rocker is nothing more than a myth. Although he did not find the Alconda for which he sought, yet a foot below the surface he got seven or eight colors to the pan and of sufficient proportions to rattle in the dish. Next year he and Dr. Kinsloe, together with Col. Hughes, will take pack horses and push onward to the spot, and are confident that a diligent search in that region may yet reveal benches of such richness and extent as to clear the memory of the Indian of being a copper colored Munchausen."[3]

INVESTIGATING THE FACTS

That, quoted as it appeared, is the story of the Lost Rocker. The fact that this tale was published in a newspaper gives it more credibility than most lost treasure stories. But, before heading for the hills in search of this fabulous bonanza, additional research is necessary.

The original newspaper account does provide us with a number of clues with which to begin our investigation. Three individuals, Mr.

---

2 Since the journey apparently began with only Jones and Hughes, these "comrades" must have been the four treasure seekers they encountered on Surprise Lake.
3 Nelson *Tribune*, December 3, 1898.

Jones, Colonel Hughes and W.D. Kinsloe, are mentioned. The lost mine was said to be near an extinct volcano, and Surprise Lake and Long Lake had to be passed en route to the location.

I decided to begin my investigation by trying to prove the existence of the three men implicated. First I examined the *B.C. Minister of Mines* index. If any of the three were involved in the goldfields of the Atlin district, particularly at the time this story was supposed to have occurred, their names might appear in one of the reports.

I did find a reference to a Tom H. Jones from the Atlin area dated 1915. It stated that a group of claims, known collectively as the "Imperial Group" was owned by W.H. Moore, James Stokes and T.H. Jones.[4] Since this was nearly 20 years after the search had been conducted for the Lost Rocker, I decided to cross-reference the Imperial Group in the index and soon learned that it had been bonded to the Nimrod Syndicate as early as 1900. "The claims are situated on the south slope of Munroe mountain, about five miles from Atlin and overlooking the valley of Pine creek."[5] The Atlin *Claim* newspaper carried a number of articles regarding the Nimrod Syndicate and its activities on Munroe Mountain in late December, 1900, but they provide no additional information. However, I subsequently learned that: "The property was first located in 1899, and in 1900 bonded to the Nimrod Syndicate. . . ."[6] Thus, "Mr. Jones" was

Thomas Jones, Atlin, June 10, 1901.

undoubtedly Tom H. Jones, and the record indicates he was still in the area a couple of years after the failed search for the treasure.

I found only one reference to a Colonel Hughes. "In February, 1899, the citizens of Atlin held a mass meeting to discuss the business affairs of Atlin, and appointed a temporary town council to look after necessary civic improvements. On the committee were L.D. Kinney, Dr. J.F. Phillips, A.J. Sammons, A.A. Douglas, G.D. Sinclair, M.R. Robinson, and Colonel A. Hughes."[7] That means that the two original men who tried to locate the lost mine did exist and were in the Atlin district about the same time. Unfortunately, I was initially unable to locate any reference to a W.D. Kinsloe.

4 B.C. *Minister of Mines*, 1914, p. 88.
5 B.C. *Minister of Mines*, 1900, p. 758.
6. D.D. Cairnes, *Memoir #37, Atlin District*, (Canada Dept. of Mines, 1913, pp. 98-100.)
7. W.W. Bilsland, "Atlin, 1898-1910: The Story of a Gold Bloom," in *B.C. Historical Quarterly*, July-October, 1952, p. 158.

The best clues to the location of the Lost Rocker Mine was its proximity to an extinct volcano. If there were indeed extinct volcanos in the Atlin district it would give additional support to the veracity of the story. As luck would have it, while researching another story in 1990-91, I came across a small newspaper article in the Klondike *Nugget* about an active volcano near Atlin. At the time, sensing it might be connected to the Lost Rocker Mine, I made a note of the date for future reference. I now decided to check out this clue and was doubly rewarded. Here is part of that article, which was datelined Tacoma, Washington, December 2, 1899:

"All the passengers of the steamer *Cottage City*, arriving from Alaska, have stories to tell of the volcano, but from Dr. W.B. Kinslowe and T.H. James, mining men of Denver who have been making an examination of the Atlin country, comes apparently the best description.

"The mountain in eruption," said D. Kinslowe, "is the second in the range of four towering peaks lying about 50 miles due south of Lake Gladios, and a shorter distance from Atlin City. Those mountains are all of at least 14,000 feet altitude, the crater resting a trifle below its three brother peaks. It was in the early part of October that the smoke was first seen issuing from the mountain. With the thought of a volcano furtherest from their minds the miners attributed these first signs of eruption to clouds hanging about the peaks.

"So constant, however, was the cloud that it became an object of daily observation from Atlin City. Then, on November 8, the mountain burst forth in flames. Through the smoke cloud there shot forth a stream of molten lava, boulders and ashes that brightened the sky for a radius of nearly 40 miles, and sent its reflected light through the darkness down upon the men working on Birch, Discovery, McKee, Pine and other creeks, the sides of whose banks face toward the volcano.

"A panic ensued among the miners when the ashes began falling down upon them. The ashes fell to a depth of several inches, and the stream down the mountain side increased in magnitude. The fall of ashes later stopped, and the men returned to work. When we left the miners were working nights, gladly profiting by the mellow twilight caused by the volcano's glare, which turned night into day. No name has yet been given the mountain, but when we left the Canadian officials at Atlin were preparing for an expedition to the volcano, and will undoubtedly name it."[8]

Researching is long, tedious work, much of it unrewarding. So you can imagine my excitement as I read this article, which gave a lot of credibility to the Lost Rocker Mine story that had appeared in the Nelson *Tribune* over one year earlier. Not only had the *Nugget* provided information about a volcano, but its reference to a "W.B. Kinslowe and T.H. James" was far too close to the W.D. Kinsloe and T.H. Jones of the trea-

8 Klondike *Nugget*, January 28, 1899.

sure story to be mere coincidence. Conceivably the *Nugget* did not spell the names correctly in its article. I have read countless old newspapers which doing research and find that spelling errors are a rather common occurrence. In fact, I have sometimes found two different spellings of the same individual in the same article, as the *Nugget* itself has done!

Although the *Nugget* story did not refer to the lost treasure, it does intimate that Kinsloe and Jones had indeed returned to the Atlin district as the original *Tribune* article said they would. The *Nugget* article also provided more information about the location of the volcano. If I could pinpoint the location of the volcano, I might be able to zero in on the site of the rich placer discovery. Unfortunately, tracking the location of the volcano is not as easy as one might expect.

In the original legend, the Indian said his discovery had been made "far back among the mountains beyond Long Lake." In trying to locate the site, according to the *Tribune*, Jones and Hughes "set out from Atlin Lake." After "reaching the head of Surprise (Lake) they portaged to Long Lake, and passed up is entire length, about 70 miles." According to the Indian, the rich placer was located on the seventh creek feeding into Long Lake. Therein lies the first problem. Where is Long Lake?

It is easy to trace the route of Jones and Hughes on any map as they made their way from Atlin Lake to Surprise Lake. However, after canoeing up Surprise Lake, they portaged to Long Lake, which was said to be 70 miles long. An examination of any map of the district will show that there is no body of water named Long Lake at the head of Surprise Lake, or, in fact, anywhere in the region. The largest lake immediately north of Surprise Lake is Gladys, but it is less than 20 miles long. Was the *Tribune* wrong about the size and was this the lake referred to as Long Lake?

Although in 1899, a 10-mile-long portage-path led from the north end of Surprise Lake to Gladys Lake,[9] I have strong doubts that this was the "Long Lake" of the original legend. First, I found no record to indicate that this lake had ever been known as Long Lake. Second, it is far from 70 miles in length. In fact, only one lake, Atlin Lake, which is 66 miles long, comes anywhere close to being the right size. In this respect, it is interesting to note that George M. Dawson once wrote that the Tagish name for this "very long lake" was A-tlin. Is it possible that the Indian had merely stated that his discovery was far back beyond the "long lake," and his comment had been misinterpreted as a body of water named "Long Lake?" Since the region was virtually unexplored at the time, it would certainly have been easy to make such a mistake.

Suppose, for the sake of argument, that Jones and Hughes had started from Surprise Lake instead of Atlin Lake. In this scenario they would head southwest along Surprise Lake and portage about 10 miles to Atlin Lake, which meant "long lake" in Tagish. According to the legend, they then followed this lake to its head and found the seventh creek that

9 *Geological Survey of Canada*, Annual Report, 1899.

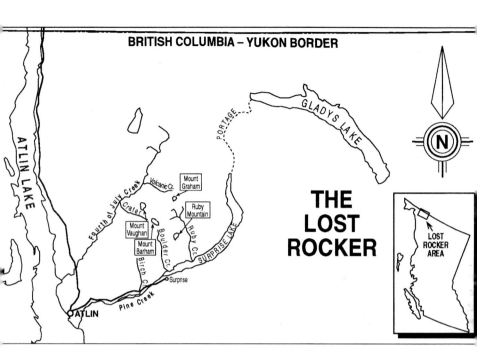

THE LOST ROCKER

entered the lake until it came to a fork. The *Tribune* article says the fork on the right inclined "toward Surprise Lake." This could only be true if they were somewhere on the northeastern shore of Atlin Lake (or, for those who favour Gladys Lake as the possible site, on the southwestern shore of that lake). The story went on to state that they choose this route because it "bore them closer to their base of supplies." This could suggest that they indeed had a base camp somewhere along Surprise Lake.

Once again the extinct volcano plays an important part. But how does it tie in with the possible locations? In the Klondike *Nugget* article, Kinslowe gave the active volcano's location as "50 miles south of Lake Gladios." This causes an immediate problem since there is no Lake Gladios located anywhere in B.C. I have to assume, therefore, that he was referring to Gladys Lake. However, additional research has led me to conclude that if there indeed was an active volcano in the Atlin district at the time, it is not the one related to the story.

After carefully studying the topographical map for the Atlin district, I located two creeks, Crater and Volcanic, that, by there very names, suggested a connection to a volcano. Located only four miles apart, both creeks flowed northwest from a group of four mountains, Ruby, Leonard, Vaughan and Barham, into Fourth of July Creek. On the southeast side of these mountains, Ruby and Boulder creeks flow into Surprise Lake, while Birch Creek flows into Pine Creek, which carries the run-off from Surprise Lake to Atlin Lake. I decided to investigate this area for

A mining scene at Pine Creek at the mouth of Willow Creek, Atlin district, c1899.

the possible existence of an extinct volcano.

In March, 1901, the Atlin *Claim* ran a series of articles written by Frank Weir on the Geology and Auriferous Deposits in Atlin District. In one of these detailed articles I found the following:

"Although part and parcel of the Auriferous belt, Ruby Creek valley may not prove of equal value, as a gold-bearing creek, with its close neighbors Birch and Boulder: for the reason that its bed is flowed with basalt, the outflow from an old volcano, whose remains, a mountain of scoria,[10] lie immediately west of the creek valley near its source."[11]

At this point I decided to visit the Provincial Archives in Victoria to learn more about extinct B.C. volcanos. Unfortunately, there was not a great deal of material available, but I did locate some additional confirmation:

"On the west side of Ruby Creek a mountain slope of brown and black scoria terminates in a crater-like summit 2,000 feet above the valley and 6,360 feet above the sea. The crater-like depression at the summit of this conical pile of scoria and basalt is about 300 yards in diameter."[12]

This entry confirmed beyond a doubt that there was as least one extinct volcano near Atlin. Whether or not it was the one mentioned in the treasure story, however, is another matter. Nevertheless, bolstered by my success to date, I decided to view the legend in its context with the known history of the region.

10 Fragmentary lava.
11. Atlin *Claim*, March 7, 1901.
12 *Geological Survey of Canada*, Annual Report, 1899, p. 303.

Gold, the reason for Atlin's existence, was discovered in the region long before the main gold rush stampede of 1899. One early newspaper reported that Russians may have been the first to mine gold in the area, and they did so as early as the 1850s. "...an old cabin has been found near the new diggings which contained the bones of a white man, presumably a Russian. Besides the remains were found an ancient rifle and a bag of gold dust weighing upwards of 70 pounds and therefore worth over £3,000. This would seem to prove that the Pine Creek placers have been known and worked many years ago."[13]

One book claims "the new-comers found old and rotten sluice boxes and other evidences showing that the former generation of miners had penetrated into this vicinity many years before,"[14] while the Atlin *Claim* reported that mining men of the district had found cabins which were at least 50 years old.[15]

In 1868, the Victoria *Colonist* published two news items related to gold discoveries in the region. The first, a despatch from Sitka dated May 28, stated that a group of miners had left for the Taku River after some Indians had reported a rich strike.[16] The second report, published on the same page, was obtained from an officer of the *USS Jamestown*, which had just arrived at Esquimalt from Sitka. This report stated that a group of Stikine miners had discovered gold on the Taku River about 70 miles northeast of Sitka. Although both discoveries were on the Taku River, they were apparently a considerable distance apart.

None of these early discoveries appear to have panned out, however, and it would be another 30 years before Fritz Miller and Kenneth McLaren would bring the Atlin goldfields to the attention of the world. But what led Miller and McLaren to the Atlin area at a time when every other prospector was hell-bent for the Klondike? Interestingly enough, the story of what led to the discovery of the Atlin goldfield dovetails nicely with the story of the Lost Rocker Mine.

"A romantic story about the arrival in Juneau of a dying prospector with a sack of gold and a rough map of his discovery led George F. Miller, the brother of Fritz, to decide upon an investigation of the area northeast of Juneau. About 1896 he ventured alone into the area supposedly shown on the map, and found some traces of gold along a waterway—later known as Pine Creek—on the eastern shore of Atlin Lake. After having several accidents and dodging Indians, of whose intentions he was uncertain, he returned to Juneau, convinced that the area which he had explored had potentialities as a gold-producing region, but also determined not to endure again the nightmarish hardships of his journey. In 1897 he and his partner, Lockie McKinnon, another long-time

13 Klondike *Nugget*, February 15, 1899.
14 E.O.S. Scholefield and F.W. and F.W. Howay, *British Columbia From the Earliest Times to the Present*, (Vancouver; 1914, Vol. II, p. 499).
15 Atlin *Claim*, March 24, 1904.
16 Victoria *Colonist*, June 8, 1868.

prospector, built the Circle City Hotel in Juneau, and there George Miller was joined by his brother and Kenneth McLaren in the winter of 1897-98. In January, 1898, when Juneau was swarming with miners bound for the Klondike discoveries, George Miller told his brother Fritz, and Fritz's partner, McLaren, about the possibilities of Pine Creek and they decided to investigate further.

"In January, 1898, in the depths of winter, Fritz Miller and McLaren set out by dog team, following the trail over the White Pass of the miners bound from Skagway to the Klondike. North of Bennett, however, they left the Klondike trail, heading east over the ice by way of Tutshi Lake and River to the Taku Arm of Tagish Lake. After travelling along Taku Arm to Graham Inlet, they followed the inlet to its head, and crossed the narrow piece of land separating them from Atlin Lake. On February 10, 1898, they landed on the frozen, silent shores of Atlin Lake. The two men found shallow deposits on Pine Creek, as George Miller had told them they would, and began work. They soon exhausted their supplies, and had to return to Jun-eau. In the summer of 1898, however, they returned and resumed their mining."[17]

George Miller first heard about gold in the Atlin district about 1896, and in that year ventured into the area alone to investigate.

On August 7, news of their discovery reached workers constructing the White Pass & Yukon Railway, and 800 lined up demanding their salary. Of the 2,000 men employed, only 700 eventually remained at the job. The rest rushed for the new gold discovery and the rest, as they say, is history.

SUMMARY AND CONCLUSION

The Nelson *Tribune*, which published the story of the Lost Rocker on December 3, 1898, stated that Jones and Hughes set out to find the site "last summer." It is unclear if the article meant the summer of 1898 or 1897, but for analysis, either year will work. The article states that Jones and Hughes had obtained information about the lost mine from an Indian who came into Juneau "several years" earlier. According to the dictionary, several is a small number "greater than two." Thus, the minimum number of years this could represent is three. If we subtract three years from 1898, we get 1895 as the year the Indian arrived at Juneau. Based on all available information, this is the latest date the Indian could have arrived in Juneau. Thus, it is entirely feasible that the prospector who first told George Miller about gold near Atlin Lake was the Indian involved in the lost treasure story. Interestingly enough, the *Tribune*, in

17 W.W. Bilsland, *op. cit.*, pp. 126-127.

(Above) Ruby Creek, near Atlin, in 1980. The remains of an extinct volcano are nearby. (Below) Mining for gold still continues in the Atlin district. This placer operation is located on Spruce Creek.

Kenneth McLaren, left, and Fritz Miller, right, c1899. After George Miller alerted his brother Fritz about gold in the Atlin district, they investigated the area, and their discoveries led to the Atlin gold rush.

its opening paragraph, suggest that there was more than one version to the Lost Rocker story. Did the other version state that it was a dying prospector who arrived in Juneau with a bag of gold? The answer to that question might lie in a faded issue of a Juneau newspaper, which I have not yet been able to access.

This lost treasure story has more credibility than many I have researched. There is a distinct possibility that the person who first supplied George Miller with information about gold near Atlin Lake was the same person involved with the lost treasure. If so, his information ultimately led to the discovery of the Atlin goldfield.

The important question then is not, did the Lost Rocker Mine ever exist, for there is a high probability that it did, but rather, is it still lost today? The answer to that question is indeed problematical. If the Lost Rocker Mine was located near the extinct volcano of Ruby Creek, there is little doubt that it was rediscovered and exhausted by the intensive mining this area has seen over the past 100 years. On the other hand, if the location of the extinct volcano referred to is actually in some obscure, little explored region northeast of Atlin, there is still a glimmer of hope. That's what so fascinating about lost treasures, it raises the meaning of that insignificant little word "if" to such monumental importance.   ❀

CHAPTER 7

DAWSON CITY'S
OUTLAW LOOT

*During one cold January morning, two masked men held-up the
Dominion Saloon and made off with $8,000 in gold dust. According
to the legend, although the culprits were eventually apprehended,
the stolen gold dust was never recovered.*

I have always been fascinated with a good treasure story, and the
one that follows really peaked my excitement for two reasons. First,
the person who related the following story was none other than
Martha Black.[1] According to Martha, she and her brother George arrived
in Skagway, Alaska, aboard the *Utopia* in June, 1898. From there, they
made their way to Dyea, then travelled over the Chilkoot Pass to Bennett
City. Three weeks later they arrived in Daw-
son, where Martha was to spend most of the
rest of her life.

In August, 1904, she married George
Black, a sourdough lawyer who had gone to
the Yukon in 1897. George became active in
Yukon politics and in the ensuing years was
elected to the Yukon council three times, once
by acclamation. In 1912 he was appointed
seventh Commissioner of the Yukon Territo-
ry, a position he held until 1916, when he
resigned to organize a Yukon Infantry Company for World War I. Following the war,
George won four successive federal elec-
tions—1921, 1925, 1926 and 1930. In 1930 he
was elected Speaker of the House of Commons. In January, 1935, because of serious ill-
ness, George resigned. This ill health prevent-

MARTHA BLACK IN 1908.

ed him from running in the next election, and it was decided that Martha
should run in his place. She was successful, and, at 69 years of age,
became only the second woman to be elected to the House of Commons.

1 Mrs. George Black, *My Seventy Years,* as told by Elizabeth Bailey Price. (Toronto; Thomas Nelson and
Sons, 1938.)

LOST BONANZAS OF WESTERN CANADA (VOL. II)
83

Interior view of the Dominion Saloon on Front Street crowded with men watching the last public gambling in Dawson. The suspension of all gambling in Dawson came as a direct result of the daring hold-up by Brophy and Tomerlin.

As an individual who had been in Dawson almost from the very beginning, Martha Black's book is often quoted in reference to that period. What made her story of the robbery even more interesting, however, was the fact that Martha had, according to her, become indirectly involved with Brophy during the period he was hiding from the law. He appeared at her cabin one morning, cold and hungry. Although she suspected he might be the fugitive, she claims to have fed him and then gave him a parcel of bread, butter, ham, tea and sugar. She also had felt sympathy for him because he had been betrayed by his partner. Here then, is Martha's account of the missing outlaw loot.

ORIGINAL LEGEND

It was during the winter of 1901 when Dawson's first and only hold-up occurred. It happened at 2 A.M. on a bitterly cold January morning with the temperature at -60° Fahrenheit. A heavy fog hung over the Yukon town like a soft grey blanket. Electric lights blinked suddenly at passers-by and as quickly winked out. Now and then footsteps crunched through the snow with ghostly sounds. Front Street, usually teeming with the night life of the dance halls, saloons and gambling joints was deserted. The terrific cold had driven most of the nighthawks to their cabins.

Listlessly the dealer at the roulette table in the old Dominion Saloon rolled the little black ball without a bet being made. Blackjack dealers

This cartoon-like depiction of the robbery appeared in the Klondike Nugget.

were making phoney bets with the boosters, who sat around waiting for suckers who failed to appear. A few miners lounged at the bar, buying occasional drinks for the dance hall girls who crowded about the huge Klondyke stove that blazed and roared until its sides glowed a dull red.

Suddenly the rear door of the saloon was flung open and two masked men stepped into the room.

"Hands up!" shouted the taller of the two, as he and his companion covered the crowd with a Winchester rifle and a pair of Colt revolvers.

Surprised by the sudden appearance of the robbers, there was nothing to do but obey. Swiftly the smaller of the two bandits emptied the cash drawer of the bar, the tills of the gambling tables, and went through the pockets of the victims. The women, frightened and whimpering, huddled together. One screamed as the short bandit approached them.

"Another yap out of you, he said with an ugly gesture of the Colt revolver, "and you'll never roll another sucker. Come through and be quick about it."

The job finished, the hold-up men backed to the door, the leader threatening, "I'll croak the first damn one of you who moves," and then they disappeared into the fog as silently as they had come.

Simultaneously, the hold-up victims leaped into action. The North West Mounted Police (NWMP) were informed, and the manhunt was on. But the desperadoes had the advantage of the fog as well as a few minutes' head start. However, if they hoped to make a clean getaway from Dawson, they would have to follow either the Yukon's up-river trail to the coast, or down river to Alaska—since a new trail in winter meant certain death.

Although the police at both boundaries were warned immediately by wire, it was impossible to send much of a description of the men, as their faces had been completely masked and they wore ordinary clothes with no distinguishing marks. The one point of agreement was that one robber was tall, the other short. Imagination was general, for violation of the law under the Canadian flag, indeed under the very noses of the NWMP, was unheard of. It simply was not done, and the thieves had no friends or sympathizers in the whole town.

A house to house search was instituted at once, and within a couple of days a tall, bland, baby-faced gentlemen, named Tomerlin, who could not give a satisfactory account of his whereabouts the night of the hold-up, was arrested by the NWMP. It was acknowledged that their efforts had been considerably assisted by information given by a dashing brunette.

Under the promise of partial immunity from punishment, Tomerlin turned King's evidence, confessed he was implicated, and surrendered his share of the loot. He said he was one of a band of three, the others being Harris and Brophy. Harris had planned the whole thing to the minutest detail, but at the last minute had lost his nerve and would not go through with it.

Disgust at the lack of loyalty of his companions undoubtedly excited the sympathy of the public for Brophy, the little bandit in some hide-out. Double-crossing a partner is not "playing the game" in the North, or as Robert Service has aptly put it, "A promise made is a debt unpaid, and the trail has its own stern code." Many were heard to say openly that they hoped that Brophy would never be captured. There were strong expressions of disapproval of Tomerlin, who had "sold out" to save himself. This might have had something to do with the fact that the search went on for months.

However, Brophy was eventually captured at the Old Stockade Roadhouse on Bonanza Creek. Returned to Dawson, he was tried, found guilty and given a life sentence. Harris got 10 years' hard labour, while Tomerlin, the informer, was deported to the United States from whence he had come.

Brophy absolutely refused to divulge where he had hidden his share of the loot, several thousand dollars in gold dust. Possibly some day some lucky person will discover the cache of jewellery, money and gold, or maybe it will remain where it was hidden until the end of time.

INVESTIGATING THE FACTS

Here, I thought upon first reading the story in Martha's book, was an unknown treasure story being revealed by someone in authority. It never occurred to me that upon closer examination of the facts the story might not "hold-up," I just wanted more details on the actual crime and information as to whether the money had ever been recovered.

My research started with the Klondike *Nugget*, and immediately I ran into a problem. Black stated the crime took place in January, 1901, so that was where I began my search. But there was no mention of any hold-up in the newspaper for January, February or March of that year. I soon came to the conclusion that she had the date of the robbery incorrect, and since I had other projects to research in other newspapers, I gave up for the moment.

When I next had the opportunity, I decided that possibly the robbery had occurred in January, 1902, and had barely started examining the newspaper for that month when a reference to Brophy and a hold-up on November 15, 1901, came to light. With this new date as a reference point, I changed microfilm rolls and quickly moved to the paper of that date, and there, on the front page, was the full details of the robbery. However, instead of reinforcing Black's story, it became immediately obvious to me that she had been grossly inaccurate in reporting the events of the robbery and subsequent capture of the robbers.

According to the *Nugget*, the hold-up occurred at 4:45 A.M. on the morning of November 15, 1901. Two men entered the gambling room of the Dominion building from a back door and ordered those inside to "throw up their hands." At the time there was only a single game of blackjack in operation, not roulette as claimed by Black. (In fact, Dawson had recently severly curtailed gambling. Only poker and blackjack was now permitted, all other forms of gambling being illegal. As a direct result of the hold-up, all forms of gambling in Dawson was outlawed within two weeks of the robbery.)

Jack Turner, one of the owners of the gambling operation, was dealing cards to Phil Wren, George McLeod, George Thompson, J.I. Dozier, and a man from the nearby creeks whose name was unknown. Along the north wall, Jack Ford was sitting at a table talking with a couple of friends, while elsewhere "a Jap was asleep on some chairs under a table." A porter was standing behind the bar. Altogether, there were only 10 or 12 people in the room, not the large crowd Black claimed and none of those present were women or dance hall girls. In fact, because of the time and the scarcity of players, the room was relatively quiet.

When the robbers first appeared, everyone thought it was a joke, and no one reacted. The second time the leader said hands up, however, they realized a robbery was taking place, and all hands promptly reached skyward. When the porter was told to join the others from the barroom, he quickly removed his wallet and hid it in the sink. He need not have concerned himself, however, as the two robbers were not interested in his money.

The apparent leader was a tall man, five feet 10 inches in height. He was wearing a dark suit of clothes, sack coat, no overcoat, a soft fur hat and held a Colt revolver in each hand. His companion was much smaller, about five feet six inches, slim, and wore a long overcoat and fur cap. He was armed with a repeating rifle. Both men wore masks made from black cloth, tied around their heads, that concealed everything but their eyes.

As soon as everyone had their hands up, the smaller man took a position in the centre of the room where he could cover them with his rifle. The leader then quickly walked over to the blackjack table and said to Turner, "Jack, give up the key to the drawer in the cashier's desk."[2]

Turner replied that the key was in the lock, upon which the robber walked over to the cage only to find out it was not there. Angered by the deception, "he hurriedly returned to the table, put one gun in his pocket and with a lightening-like sweep of the palm of his free hand cocked the gun he still held, showing an unmistakable familiarity with weapons and their rapid use, and said. 'Hand over that key, Jack. I don't want any monkey business this time or I'll turn this joint into a slaughterhouse'."

Turner surrendered the key and the leader returned to the cashier's desk and opened the till. In an instant he had scooped out the contents and placed them in his left outside coat pocket. He then joined his companion and, keeping the room covered with their weapons, they backed out the same door they had entered and disappeared.

The robbers had barely gone out the back door when several people ran out the front way to spread the alarm. However, by the time they circled the block to the alley there was no trace of the bandits. It was at first thought that they had made their escape by passing through one of the restaurants behind the Dominion and exiting on Second Avenue. But employees of the Great Northern, Columbia and Joe Juneau's restaurants were certain no one had passed through their

Det. McGuire, above, and Corp. Piper, below, with the assistant of an informer, soon captured the two robbers. The photo of Sgt. Piper was taken in 1912.

2 All quotes are taken directly from the newspaper accounts.

kitchen at the time of the robbery.

Herman Schradle, proprietor of the Mocha chop house restaurant, later stated that he had witnessed two men answering the description of the robbers arguing in the alley about 4:30 A.M. They appeared to be angry about something. The taller man was being abusive to the other and Schradle though there was going to be a fight.

Jack Ford told a *Nugget* reporter that the taller man, "who did all the talking was as cool as you please, not the least excited. He knew what he was about, perfectly, and must have

This sketch of Matt Tomerlin appeared in the Klondike Nugget.

been thoroughly familiar with the premises as well as the surroundings. He must also have been acquainted with Turner. . .as he called him 'Jack'." Contradicting Black's account, he added: "The little fellow who stood guard did not utter a sound all the time they were in the room."

Sergeant Smith of the NWMP was on the scene within minutes of the robbery and carefully examined the alley for clues, but without success.

It must have come as quite a surprise to Dawson residents when, the very next day, the *Nugget* reported that Sergeant Smith, Corp. John Piper and Detective McGuire had taken into custody Matt Tomerlin in connection with the robbery. This was prompt action on the part of the police who, except for the heights of the robbers, had no clues to go on. However, a possible reason for the prompt arrest surfaced later in the newspaper account when it was reported that "there were three partners in the hold-up enterprise and when the 'divy' was made there was not an equal 'cut,' and in consequence the third party 'piped' on the other two and that the police, having a straight 'tip,' had nothing to do (but) go to Tomlin's (sic) room and arrest him."

Although the report was denied, this was essentially what had happened, although it would be quite some time before the full details were released.

The robbery had been planned and was to have been executed by three men, Edwin Harris, William Brophy and Matt Tomerlin. However, the day before the robbery, Harris "got cold feet and backed out." Between 9 and 10 o'clock on the morning following the robbery, the three men met in front of the Monte Carlo. Harris was "excited and nervous for some reason and did not seem as if he wanted to see us," Tomerlin later testified.

Harris had good reason to be nervous, for only an hour or so earlier

The Great Northern Hotel, shown here in 1898, was one of the possible targets selected for robbery by Brophy, Tomerlin and Harris.

he had advised Albert Beebe, an employee at the Dominion, that he knew who had committed the robbery, identifying the robbers as Brophy and Tomerlin. Beebe advised Harris to go see Detective McGuire, which he did. As a result of information obtained from Harris, around 5 P.M. on the day of the robbery, McGuire, Sergeant Smith and Corporal Piper visited Tomerlin in his room in the Webb Building. Armed with a search warrant, they began to look for evidence. While doing this another man arrived who fit the description of the second robber, and, upon identifying himself as Brophy, he was advised by Smith that they also had a warrant to search his cabin.

After locating two revolvers that appeared to match the description of those used in the robbery, Tomerlin was arrested. Nothing was found in Brophy's cabin to implicate him, but later that day he was also arrested for suspicion of robbery. The preliminary hearing of Matt Tomerlin was held on November 30, 1901. At this hearing, no mention was made of Harris having implicating Tomerlin, and all the evidence presented was circumstantial. Nevertheless, Tomerlin was bound over for trial. At his next appearance, on December 14, Tomerlin pleaded not guilty and elected trial by jury.

The police had even less evidence with which to convict Brophy of robbery, so on December 2 he was formerly charged instead with being a "loose, idle and disorderly person."

At Brophy's trial two days later, the first witness was Jack Turner's brother Thomas. He testified that he had known Brophy for months, and during that period had on several occasions hired him as a "booster" at the Dominion's blackjack table. Brophy was supplied with stacks of chips and instructed to make the game look lively by betting two chips on every hand dealt. For this service he was paid $6 a day. Jack Turner testified to practically the same thing. Neither man knew Brophy to be otherwise employed.

However, Edwin Harris, who had implicated Brophy in the robbery in the first place, testified that he knew Brophy to be a good quartz miner who was able to command 50¢ per day more than ordinary hardrock miners. This was reinforced by Frank Beckel, who testified to having known Brophy since 1897 when he worked with him in the Glacier mine near Juneau. These testimonies, plus the fact that Brophy had $19 on him when arrested, was sufficient to win his acquittal on the vagrancy charge. Brophy then promptly disappeared.

Then, on December 28, Tomerlin confessed to everything. He had been the tall robber and Brophy had been his shorter accomplice. But Tomerlin claimed that Harris, whose testimony had helped clear Brophy, was the ringleader. Clearly, this is not supported by the mass of evidence and testimony that later came out. But the police had seen one of the robbers slip through their fingers for lack of evidence and they offered Tomerlin immunity from prosecution if he testified against his accomplices.

There is no doubt that Harris had planned the robbery with Brophy and Tomerlin. There is also little doubt that Tomerlin was the gang leader. Yet, by testifying against his accomplices, he escaped justice for his crime, just as he had done once before in Nome, Alaska. Harris, on the other hand, never actually participated in the robbery, and in fact had voluntarily admitted to police that he had been involved in the planning before backing out. He also directed police to the perpetrators, who very likely would never have been caught without his help.

Following his trial, Harris was remanded to jail without sentencing by Judge Dugas. On March 15, 1902, the Klondike *Daily Nugget* reported: "In the Harris case there are legal points involved which his lordship stated he did not care to pass upon, but instead would send a reserve to the Supreme Court of Canada and leave it to that tribunal whether or not the accused should be convicted."

A week later, however, Harris was brought back before Judge Dugas who pronounced him guilty as charged. However, sentence was suspended pending the decision of the higher court.

Of the three, Brophy's punishment would be the most severe. First, of course, he had to be apprehended. Brophy eluded capture until February 26, 1902. After learning that the fugitive had been seen in the vicinity of the Stockade Roadhouse at 19 Below Discovery on Bonanza Creek, constables Egan and McMillan were assigned to watch the area.

On the evening of his capture they saw a man answering Brophy's description enter the roadhouse. Positioning themselves on either side of the door, they waited. About a half hour later, Brophy was tackled as he exited the building in the dark. During the struggle, Egan saw Brophy raise his arm and thought he had a knife or revolver. Pressing the muzzle of his revolver into Brophy's side, Egan fired. Brophy was then subdued and, after his wound was attended to by the police doctor at Grand Forks, he was returned to Dawson. Following his trial, it took the jury only 14 minutes to find him guilty, whereupon Judge Dugas said: "The sentence of the court is that you be imprisoned at hard labor for the rest of your life."

SUMMARY AND CONCLUSION

This brings us to the several thousand dollars in jewellery, money and gold dust, which, according to Martha Black was never recovered. For details of what was actually taken during the hold-up, I refer to the Klondike *Nugget* of November 15, 1901, the very day of the robbery, when it reported:

"The booty secured by the robbery consisted of gold and silver coins, gold dust and nuggets, the total value of which, as stated by Mr. Turner this morning, amounts to $1,401. In the same drawer was a $500 roll of bills which in the excitement was overlooked. The money was the property of the Turner Bros., Jack and Tom, who have the gambling privileges in the Dominion. No effort was made to go through any of those present, nor was the drawer of the black jack table, which contained about $200, molested. Just at the time the robbers appeared one of the players had cashed in $85, the money being still on the table when the taller one walked over to Turner after the key. It was in a position that he could not have helped but see it, yet he did not take it."

It is quite apparent from this newspaper report that, contrary to what Black wrote in her book, the robbers did not "empty the tills of the gambling tables" or go "through the pockets of the victims." Also contrary to Black's account, no women were said to have been in attendance from which jewellery could be stolen.

At Brophy's trial, which began on March 11, Thomas Turner presented a detailed accounting of the money stolen. There was "$841 in currency, $106 in nuggets, $35 in gold coin, $393 in gold dust and $46 in silver." This totalled $1,401. However, Turner also testified that the $46 is silver was not taken, making the actual amount of the theft $1,355. This is considerably less that the $8,000 reported as having been taken by Black. Of the original $1,355, how much, if any, was recovered?

As already mentioned, because of Harris, Tomerlin and Brophy were arrested within hours of the robbery. When the police first visited Tomerlin's room, he professed to be broke and 10 days in arrears in his rent. However, Constable Jackson, who had also been present, testified that some money had been found in his pockets, "and in a belt concealed under his trousers was over $600 in currency." Whether or not this currency was part of the robbery loot was never clarified in court.

During Tomerlin's confession on December 28, he told police where they had hidden the clothes and weapons used in the robbery. Tomerlin then led authorities to the residence of E.B. Condon. Following the robbery, Brophy and Tomerlin had crawled under the house and concealed the stolen loot. Pointing out the spot, "$390 in currency together with the dust and nuggets was recovered. An effort was made to find Brophy's cache, but it was unsuccessful, and it is concluded by the detectives to have been 'lifted' long ere this."

Since Turner identified the nuggets stolen from the Dominion and produced in court by the police, and since at least $390 in currency was also recovered, the whereabouts of only $451 in currency and $35 in gold coins remains in question. That does not mean, however, that they were not recovered, only that they are unaccounted for in the newspaper accounts.

It is quite obvious that Brophy returned to the Condon residence and removed his share of the loot after he had been found not guilty of vagrancy. That was on December 3, 1901. Brophy was subsequently captured on February 26, nearly three months later. There is no testimony to indicate how much money, if any, was found on Brophy when he was captured. However, even if he was broke, it is not far fetched to assume that he had spent the money during the period he was hiding out from police. During the first three weeks of the police manhunt, for instance, Brophy had been staying in a Dawson hotel. He then went to Grand Forks in the company of a woman, and there disappeared. Later his movements were tracked to the Stockade Roadhouse.

In my opinion, it is very unlikely that any part of the outlaw loot remains hidden. After retrieving the money from Condon's residence, it seems ludicrous that Brophy would hide it elsewhere. The reason for concealing the loot in the first place was to avoid getting caught with stolen goods. However, with Tomerlin's confession, everyone knew Brophy was guilty and would be arrested on sight, and whether he possessed part of the stolen loot on his person made no difference. �֍

CHAPTER 8

SLOCAN LAKE'S
LOST SILVER BULLION

*According to the legend, a boxcar loaded with silver bullion,
rolling with the motion of the barge during a storm, smashed through
the guard rails and vanished into the dark waters below.*

T HE first man known to have searched for minerals in the Slocan
region of British Columbia was Robert Baird. In 1884 Baird,
accompanied by an Indian, prospected the creeks of the Slocan in
search of placer gold. In one of the creeks near the future town-site of
Three Forks, he found traces of gold, but not in paying quantities. Dis-
couraged, Baird left the area and made his way to East Kootenay where
he gained employment with Eddy, Hammond & Company. That
November, while transporting the company's receipts to Montana, he
was bushwhacked and murdered by Bull Dog Kelly 24 miles south of
Golden.[1]

Two years later Capt. George Sanderson, Jack Evans and an
unnamed German made their way into the Slocan by way of the as yet
unnamed Carpenter Creek. Like Baird, they were searching for placer

1 See "Bulldog Kelly's Buried Loot," starting on page 33 of this book.

gold; and like Baird, they also made their way inland as far as Three Forks. Plenty of galena was found, but it was considered worthless at the time and the discovery was ignored. This party then also left the region.[2]

It was not until the summer of 1891 that the richness of Slocan's treasure vault would begin to surface. It all began when three prospectors, Andrew Jardine, John Allen and Jack McDonald found a promising outcrop of silver in the Blue Ridge Mountains about 13 miles up Kaslo Creek and staked the Beaver claim. In August, Jardine returned to Ainsworth, on Kootenay Lake, with a quantity of high-grade silver-lead ore. Prompted by this discovery, a number of prospectors decided to investigate the area. Among them were Eli Carpenter and John L. Seaton, and it was their discovery that put the Silvery Slocan on the map.[3]

By early September, Seaton and Carpenter found themselves within sight of Slocan Lake. Although they had penetrated further westward than the other prospectors, their search thus far had been unsuccessful, so the two men decided to return to Ainsworth. At this point Seaton and Carpenter apparently split up; Seaton headed east while Carpenter headed west for Slocan Lake.

According to the February 4, 1894 issue of the Nelson *Tribune:* "In retracing his steps, Seaton discovered the outcroppings of the Payne mine. While engaged in staking the claim he was overtaken by Carpenter, who had changed his mind regarding the route out." The date was September 9, 1891, and the Payne was the first location to be made in the soon to be famous Silvery Slocan. Seaton and Carpenter then hurried back to Ainsworth to have their specimens assayed.[4]

Although the true sequence of events that transpired after the two

2 Garnet Basque, *West Kootenay: The Pioneer Years,* (Langley; Sunfire Publications, 1990, p. 93.)
3 *Ibid.,* p. 93.
4 *Ibid.,* p. 96.

First known as Eldorado, New Denver sprang into existence on the shore of Slocan Lake when rich silver-producing mines were discovered nearby.

(Above) A general view of Sandon, and its two railroads, in 1896.
(Opposite page) According to the legend, a boxcar loaded with silver bullion, being shunted by barge down Slocan Lake to Slocan City, overturned during a storm and sank.
(Opposite page, inset) Don W. Hird, mayor of Slocan City from 1962-80, worked on one of the salvage attempts.

men reached Ainsworth will probably never be known, most historians suggest that Carpenter tried to swindle Seaton out of his discovery.[5] Carpenter, accompanied by E.A. Bielenberg, left for Slocan River by way of Nelson. A week later, a furious Seaton led a party of about 20 prospectors into the area by a shorter, more direct route. The Seaton party reached the site first, and on October 5, 1891, Seaton, Jack and Bill Hennessey, Frank Flint and Jack McGuigan staked a group of claims known as the Noble Five. Before the year ended, 191 claims had been staked, most of them in the snow.

During the summer of 1892 the woods were crawling with prospectors, while mines like the Slocan Star, Freddie Lee, Noble Five, Payne, Reco and Wonderful began to produce. At first the ore was taken to Kaslo, a new town that sprang up on Kootenay Lake, 30 miles from the mines, by pack mules. The trail was rough and it proved to be a time-consuming and inefficient means of transporting the ore. But that was all about to change.

Following the discoveries in the Slocan, a small town began to take shape on Slocan Lake at the mouth of Carpenter Creek. In mid-January 1892, New Denver, known initially as Eldorado, had only a general store, operated by Hunter & Co., and four cabins. By April fully 500 men were camped in the neighbourhood of Eldorado and some 50 buildings had been erected. Two months later a trail had been completed from the new

5 This is covered in detail in *West Kootenay: The Pioneer Years*, pp. 96-97.

town into the very heart of the silver country. Two-thirds shorter than the trail to Kaslo, it soon became the preferred transportation route.

Attracted by the rich silver-producing mines of the Slocan, the Canadian Pacific Railway (CPR) constructed a branch line south from Nakusp, on Arrow Lake, to its terminus at Three Forks. Known as the Nakusp and Slocan (N&S), this railway had one major drawback: ore had to be hauled down to the railhead from Sandon in wagons, a distance of four miles. This opened the door for a second railway, and in March, 1895, the Kaslo and Slocan (K&S) began construction in Kaslo with a terminus in Sandon. Faced by this challenge, the N&S decided to push into Sandon itself.

For a number of years the silver-producing mines around Sandon had two railways by which to ship their ore. Gradually, however, the N&S, with its ties to the CPR, began to enjoy the greater portion of the business.

ORIGINAL LEGEND

The CPR, through its stern-wheeler and barge system, was able to provide an efficient delivery system. Ore headed south was shipped by boxcar to Rosebery, just north of New Denver. Here the heavily-laden boxcars were placed on a barge, which was shunted by stern-wheelers like the *Slocan* down Slocan Lake to Slocan City. At Slocan City the barge was unloaded and the boxcars continued their trip to the smelter at Trail or other destinations.

According to T.W. Paterson, the system worked well enough until the winter of 1904, "when a boxcar belonging to the Consolidated Mining and Smelting Company, and loaded not with silver ore, but with silver bars, was lost during a storm. The heavily-laden car, rolling with the motion of the barge, had begun rolling along its tracks to the edge of the barge, where it smashed through the guard rails and vanished into the dark waters.

"Soundings indicated the boxcar to be resting on a steep slope in less than 100 feet of water, although this was subject to change should currents or salvage attempts dislodge the car from its precarious perch.

"Despite fears that the bullion might slip deeper into the murky depths, company officials were optimistic and brought in professional 'hard-hat' divers who assured them that the operation should be relatively straight-forward. After several reconnaissance dives, the salvors decided that, rather than risk losing the car, which was canted sharply on its side, by trying to remove its cargo, it would be best to raise the boxcar with bullion intact.

"All went according to plan, the divers successfully rigging the car to a barge and, at a signal, crewman began winching the treasure to the surface. Time passed, with only the cables, taut as violin strings, rippling the surface of the lake as the winches protested shrilly. But, slowly, surely, the cables were coiled around their drums aboard the salvage barge and finally a swirling of green water indicated that the boxcar was just inches from the surface.

"Seconds later, water and mud pouring from its undercarriage, the bullion car rose from the water, the ecstatic salvors cheering its appearance. But their celebration changed to tears when, as they were maneuvering a second barge under the swaying freight car, a cable, stretched to its breaking point, let go with a crack, plunging the boxcar onto the barge's bow.

"As the heart-broken salvors watched, the treasure-laden car ruptured, then, in a swirl of white, disappeared into the depths once more. When divers again descended to the Slocan's muddy bottom, they reported that the boxcar, now broken in half, much of its cargo undoubtedly buried in the silt, had come to rest at a greater depth than its original resting place. They had been beaten."

According to Paterson, 30 years passed before treasure hunters again tried to salvage "Slocan Lake's lost silver bars." During the depression another Vancouver diving firm tried to recover the silver. As before, "a diver, ungainly in hard hat, air hose and suit, clambered over the side of a barge and vanished beneath the lake's surface. Armed with explicit instructions as to the boxcar's location, he found it easily enough in the gloom, it apparently not having been disturbed since the accident.

Wearing cumbersome underwater gear similar to this, a diver identified only as Moore, located the submerged boxcar two months after the accident and, according to the local newspaper, recovered most of the copper bars.

After carefully surveying its ghostly remains, the diver concluded that the silver had not been spilled when the freight car split in two, but remained intact, in one-half of the car.

"His hunch proved correct, when, groping through the silt, and aware that the slightest careless move could cause the listing wreck to shift, crushing him, the diver felt a jumble of solid objects. Working blindly in the murk, he cautiously dragged one of the lumps from its fellows and secured it to a hawser. At his signal, the invisible object glided upward, his surface crew jubilantly reporting it to be a silver ingot!

"Thus heartened, the diver proceeded to extricate one bar after another, relying upon his sense of touch to locate the unseen treasure. Making his difficult task almost impossible was the overwhelming

(Above) A railroad barge of more recent vintage was tied up at the Rosebery slip when visited by the author in July, 1896. The tug is the Iris G.
(Opposite page) An aerial view of Slocan City in August, 1984. According to Irvin Anderson, who worked on some of the more modern salvage attempts, and once operated the tug Iris G. *seen above, the ill-fated barge sank approximately where the logs are seen in this photo.*

knowledge that, at any moment, the shattered freight car could roll. Even if he escaped being crushed, he knew that his lifeline could not fail to be entangled, or cut, in the boxcar's jagged edges. If the car should decide to continue its descent along the sloping lake bottom, he knew, he was a dead man.

"It was this unnerving threat which finally ended his venture. Although the bulk of the silver bullion remained, the salvors had reputedly recovered two dozen of the precious ingots.

"Encouraged by this second, successful, attempt at salvage, others soon tried their hands at outwitting Slocan Lake. But despite the use or modern, and expensive, equipment, these latter-day treasure hunts have failed. Over the years, the dismembered boxcar has moved, and the lake bottom has shifted. Making matters worse is the fact that recent surveys indicate that both halves of the ill-fated boxcar are now empty, the heavy bars having poured into the mud during the upheavals underwater. This theory seems to have been confirmed by reports that a dredge accidentally hauled up several of the long-sought bars when working in the area.

"Whatever the case, Slocan Lake continues to hold its silver treasure."

INVESTIGATING THE FACTS

The above story of Slocan Lake's lost silver bullion was written by T.W. Paterson and appeared in *Canadian Treasure Trails*, a book published by Stagecoach Publishing in 1976. When the first edition of *Lost Bonanzas of Western Canada* was published by Sunfire Publications in 1983, the story was included virtually unchanged. However, when I decided to do a new updated and enlarged version in 1988, I decided not to include this particular story. That decision was based on my not having personally investigated the facts of the story, and, if you noticed, Paterson did not mention any sources whatsoever to indicate where he got his information. This made my job even more difficult.

I decided to begin my research into this story by reading the newspapers of the day. The first newspaper I read, the New Denver *Ledge*, failed to turn up anything of interest. I then turned to the *Slocan Drill*. It did not contain any information about a boxcar loaded with silver bullion having gone down in Slocan Lake. However, it did contain several news items that I found very interesting.

"One of the most unfortunate fatalities in the history of the camp occurred here on Tuesday night (December 22, 1903), E.O. Conley, a C.P.R. brakeman, being the victim. About midnight a freight train arrived in to run the transfer barge. Conductor Wansley and Engineer Govett being in charge. After unloading the barge, the train crew began filling it up again with cars to be transferred north. The end of these cars was freighted with copper bullion, consigned from Smelter Junction to San Francisco. Conley was on top of the car setting the brakes, but the momentum gained was so great that the car went over the barge into deep water, carrying the poor fellow with him.

"Conley was heard to call for help when falling, but on striking the water he disappeared, the suction from the sinking car pulling him down. The balance of the train crew rushed to the scene and did everything they could to rescue their comrade, but without avail. They and a number of citizens worked until almost daylight to recover the body, but without result. They found the resting place of the car, and the body is supposed to be beneath it. Where the accident occurred there is about 50 feet of water. No blame can be attached to anyone for the unfortunate accident.

"The drowned man was about 21 years of age and had been working with that train crew for about a month, running out of Nelson. Practically nothing is known of his friends or where he came from. The car of bullion was valued at upwards of $4,000 and the railway company will send in equipment to recover the treasure, when the body may also be found. The hardness of the world was to be noticed the next day, when the bridge crew anchored their barge over the fatal spot and resumed the driving of piles for repairing the slip. But such is life."[6]

6 *Slocan Drill*, December 25, 1903.

If this article is in fact the nucleus from which the "lost silver bullion" story originated, and I have a strong suspicion that it is, then there are some glaring errors and omissions in the original legend. First and foremost, of course, the shipment, according to the newspaper, was "copper bullion," not "silver bullion." This, of course, would dramatically decrease the value of any unrecovered treasure. Also, Paterson claims the boxcar sank out on Slocan Lake during a storm, while in fact, the boxcar merely overran the barge while being loaded and sank near the shore. An error of omission is the fact that a man lost his life and that is not mentioned in the original legend.

The first article that appeared in the newspaper has already provided us with a great deal of information about the lost treasure. A month later we learn a little more. "The railway company has made no effort as yet to recover the car of bullion lost over the slip here, nor has it shown any disposition to find the body of the poor brakeman drowned at the time."[7]

On Tuesday evening, February 9, a diver named Moore arrived from Vancouver with a helper and diving apparatus. He descended for the first time on Wednesday afternoon, while a large crowd of spectators watched. Although Moore "ran across cartrucks lost a year or so ago," reported the newspaper, he was unable to locate the missing bullion car. He also found no trace of Conley, the drowned brakeman.[8]

A week later Moore was successful in his search.

"An unusual scene of entertainment has been provided by the operations of diver Moore during the week. He located the lost car and got to work on it Friday. It was found broken in two and held by the truss rods, but with no bullion in either end. Cables were fastened to the car, but the steam winch was not powerful enough to lift it from the mud. All told about 700 bars of bullion were in the car when lost, and the majority of these have been recovered. The lantern of the dead brakeman was found, but nothing was seen of the body of the poor fellow."[9]

SUMMARY AND CONCLUSION

A short time after this story appeared in the summer 1993 issue of *Canadian West* magazine, I received a letter from Irvin M. Anderson, one of the subscribers. Anderson worked on the Slocan Lake tug and barge system for 22 years. He started as a deckhand on the *Ss Rosebery* in 1953. When the old steamship was retired in 1956, it was replaced by the diesel tug *Iris G*, which can be seen in the photograph on page 100. In 1969 Anderson purchased Interior Lake Service and operated the *Iris G.* with a deckhand until he sold out in 1975.

According to Anderson, "the exact location of the car on which E.O. Conely (Conally?) rode to his death over the barge's end stop is about

7 *Slocan Drill*, January 29, 1904.
8 *Slocan Drill*, February 12, 1904.
9 *Slocan Drill*,February 19, 1904.

midway between the end of the barge and the log boom" in the photograph on page 101. "It was common practice for the train crews to make 'flying switches' in the yard and an old brakeman told me that this is what happened. Conely, young and inexperienced, did not anticipate the steeper grade toward the slipway.

"Don Hird, a former mayor of Slocan City and still a resident there at 84 years of age, told me that he helped worked the compressor pumps in 1929 for one MacDougall who had contracted to extend the slipway and had a diver who attempted to salvage the remaining 100 or more bars. He recalls MacDougall shutting down the operation while he took some of the salvaged ingots back to town on the train. When he returned he closed down the seemingly successful operation without explanation."[10]

Don Hird's involvement was first mentioned in a letter I received from Irvin Anderson dated July 26, 1993. After I wrote him requesting photographs of individuals involved in the salvage attempts, Anderson wrote a second letter dated October 16, 1993. In this letter he stated: "I talked to Don Hird on the phone this morning and he tells me that when he worked for MacDougall on the salvage job in '29 that 38 small 'high grade bullion' bars of silver and gold were recovered. Each was about 20" long and that the rest were left since they were of low grade lead."[11]

Getting back to Anderson's first letter, he continued: "However, higher silver prices in the sixties induced more salvage efforts. A diving friend of mine (Bill Hook of Victoria) had no problem locating the car resting on a 45 degree plus slope in 60 or 80 feet of water. It appeared to be broken in two and he was puzzled by a huge mound of silt that had almost half buried it. I recalled from the old Ss *Rosebery* days that the firemen used to dump their ashes above this location. Bill was not interested in salvage but did say it would require some thought to get rid of this accumulation.

"Enter a local mining man entrepreneur extra ordinem in the person of Alex Seminick, and this is when our crew became involved. First of all he hired a helicopter to hover a 'silver-finding' dowser chap over the area to pinpoint the exact location of the treasure. For several days after our regular work for the CPR we re-spotted the barge for his suction-compression equipment and tied it in position. Once he engaged us to pull the trucks of the car to deeper water where we chopped the cables to release them.

"But, as suddenly as the interest had spawned so it died. A rumour circulated that some bars had been recovered but it was wondered why the job had not been completed and why the sudden secrecy or news blackout of the operation?

"The last attempt to recover the bars (to my knowledge) was made since 1975 after my tenure on the lake. Now, modern divers with light,

10 Letter from Irvin Anderson dated July 26, 1993.
11 Letter from Irvin Anderson dated October 16, 1993.

Capt. A.D. Osis of Slocan City, with a "lead" bar recovered from the last salvage attempt on the sunken boxcar.

sophisticated equipment supposedly found the car and a few bars still on the floor. They brought up three and took them to Trail for assay. They apparently tried to research old CPR records but ran into a stone wall since records had been lost or misplaced, etc. Each bar weighed about 80 lbs. and had TADANAC stamped on them. They were pure lead!

"So a mystery still surrounds the actual content of that ill fated car. Perhaps it was a mixed shipment of silver, lead and copper. Sources seem to agree that the original salvage was highly successful with the recovery of seven-eights or more of the shipment two or more months after the incident.

One of the bars was given to the proprietor of the Inn at that time and the other to my old friend and skipper Adolph Osis of Slocan for his help and cooperation in assisting these chaps as to the correct location. Which brings me to another story of Slocan Lake which Paterson obviously heard and integrated into his bullion fable.

"Adolph was a deckhand on the *Ss Rosebery* the early morning of January 1, 1947, when one of the old wooden barges, #18[12] to be exact, on which was loaded the engine #3512, caboose, snowplow and three boxcars of lumber, listed outboard from the ship and slid into the lake taking the tracks and hog posts (upright support structure of wooden barges) with them. The location of the sinking is approximately half way down the page on the left hand margin of your excellent picture on page 97. Had there been enough steam in the locomotive, which had been loaded

12 In Anderson's letter of October 16, 1993, after discussing this incident with Adolph Osis, Osis stated that the two barges involved with #5 and #14.

several hours earlier, the engine could have been moved ahead and while sacrificing the loads on that side may have stabilized the barge enough until the suction pumps could escape the water. These pumps were steam operated and while the large one, had it been used, may have averted the disaster, the firemen and engineers hated it because it cut down drastically on operating pressure. So, they used the small one! After all it was New Year's Day and all hands were anxious to be home."[13]

Although there are a number of the inconsistencies and discrepancies between the original legend, written by Paterson, and the newspapers accounts, I am convinced they both concern the same mishap. Since Paterson gave no sources of references from where he obtained his information, I must assume the newspaper accounts that appeared in the *Slocan Drill* are basically accurate. Thus it would appear the lost treasure happened this way.

On December 22, 1903, a boxcar loaded with about 700 bars of copper was being loaded onto a barge at Slocan City. A brakeman was riding on top of the boxcar to apply the brakes, but the boxcar's momentum was so great that it continued through the guard rail, taking the brakeman to his death. To the best of my knowledge, his body was never recovered.

In mid-February, 1904, a salvage attempt was made on the submerged boxcar and its load of copper bullion by a Vancouver diver identified only as Moore. Moore was able to locate the boxcar and attach cables to it. However, the steam derrick was not powerful enough to lift it from the lake's bottom. Nevertheless, Moore was able to recover most of the copper bars.

If we accept the facts of the incident as reported in the *Slocan Drill*, then we must also accept the fact that the bullion was copper, not silver, and most of it was recovered two months after the accident. However, the two letters from Anderson do cause a bit of a mystery. If he is correct, and the boxcar did indeed included bars of silver, copper and lead, it leaves us with two possibilities. Either the CPR misinformed the newspaper about the cargo to prevent unauthorized salvage attempts or the newspaper made an error. The *Slocan Drill*, which identified the cargo as "copper," did so only once, on December 25, 1903. Thereafter, it referred to the cargo simply as "bullion." Was this because it was indeed a mixed-cargo? If, as Anderson states, the records of the incident have been lost or misplaced, we will probably never know the answer. However, there is one aspect of this treasure in which we can remain relatively certain: most of the bars have been recovered over the years. There may still be a few copper or lead bars lying in the bottom of Slocan Lake, but I hardly think it can still be considered a worthwhile "treasure."   ❀

---

13 Letter from Irvin Anderson dated July 26, 1993.

CHAPTER 9

THE LOST STRONGBOX
OF THE MOUNT ROYAL

Ever since she sank in Kitselas Canyon on July 6, 1907, rumours
have persisted that the Mount Royal's *safe went to the bottom*
containing as much as $100,000 in gold.

KITSELAS Canyon, on the Skeena River about 10 miles east of Terrace, British Columbia, was once described by an early traveller as "the most justly dreaded inland waterway of the Northwest, for, aside from the tremendous force of the contracted river over an uneven rocky bottom, forming great swirls and riffles, the upper entrance is obstructed by two high, narrow, rock ridges that divide the waters, forming two narrow channels at all stages and a third at extreme high water. The walls on either hand are precipitous or strewn with immense boulders to a height of 50 to 100 feet, where narrow benches slope back from them to the mountains 3,000 to 4,000 feet in altitude."[1]

This part of the Skeena River was once dominated by the Canyon Tsimshian, the Kitselas. Nothing passed up or down the river without their permission, and without paying a toll. The first white men to challenge their supremacy was the Collins Overland Telegraph Company in 1866. At first the Kitselas refused to allow them passage, but upon being told that the men were not traders, and seeing that they were heavily armed, they not only relented, but assisted them in pulling their laden canoes through the canyon.

"Although their hold in the Canyon had been challenged, it wasn't till the Omineca Gold Rush that it was finally broken; by the early 70's, miners were streaming up the Skeena to the new eldorado. Many of the Kitselas made money taking canoes through the canyon; however, they no longer controlled the river."[2]

By the turn of the century the four Tsimshian villages at Kitselas Canyon, Tsune-ee-yow, Kit-lak-soak, Kit-Ousht and Kit-lth-Sahok, were deserted. "Where once 1,000 Kitselas Indians had lived, controlling the

1 Quoted by Ed Kenney in "Kitselas—Gateway to the Past," an article in *Skeena Digest*, date unknown, p. 7 & 9.
2 Ed Kenny, "Kitselas—Gateway to the Past," *Skeena Digest*, p. 9.

(Above) An early coloured postcard view of the junction of the Skeena and Bulkley rivers. (Opposite page) The Mount Royal *leaving Port Essington.*

The Main Street of Kitselas c1912.

canyon, there were now only empty lodges and decaying totem poles. Most of the people had moved to the Coast to fish or work in the canneries since the white man had changed the traditional life in the Canyon. A few, about 60, moved four miles down river and built a new village, Andee-dom, or Newtown."[3]

As more white settlers moved into the area, some to homestead, Kitselas became a focal point. New buildings were constructed on the site of the old Indian village of Kit-Ousht. First the Hudson's Bay Company (HBC) built a warehouse, and in 1907, J.W. Patterson built a store which doubled as a post office.

Meanwhile, trade on the Skeena River had intensified. The two main centres were at Port Essington, near the river's mouth, and Hazelton, 180 miles upriver. Initially, freight between these two points were transported by canoe; but this was time-consuming and expensive, especially on the upriver run.

To correct the problem, the HBC hired Capt. George Odin, of New Westminster, to survey the Skeena, especially the treacherous Kitselas Canyon. Based on his favourable report, the HBC constructed a sternwheeler named the *Caledonia* in 1890. In May, 1891, under Captain Odin, this vessel made the first successful trip up the Skeena River to Hazelton. Although the journey took nine days, it ushered in a new era of transporting freight.

The *Caledonia* served northern coastal waters for seven years. Then

3 *Ibid*, p. 9.

in 1898 her machinery was removed and installed in a new stern-wheeler of the same name.

The HBC's main competitor on the Skeena River was an ex-employee named Robert Cunningham. Since leaving the HBC, Cunningham had founded Port Essington, and started a variety of business ventures from salmon canneries to lumber mills. For years Cunningham had been content to transport goods by canoe. In 1900, however, he decided to enter the freight business in direct competition with the HBC. To accomplish this, Cunningham first purchased the stern-wheeler Monte Cristo, then promptly hired Captain Bonser from the HBC. Everyone now anticipated a strong rivalry to develop, but with their new vessel, the *Strathcona*, the HBC felt that they could easily compete, so they simply ignored their former employees.

"Cunningham, however, was not through yet. That same winter he sent Captain Bonser to Victoria to design a stern-wheeler especially for the Skeena, and by the spring of 1901 the *Hazelton* was ready. During the first season she made 13 trips to Hazelton, steaming up river in 40 hours and returning in 10. The HBC were no longer competitive, and to meet this challenge, they built the *Mount Royal*. The intense rivalry everyone had expected was now on."[4]

Named after the chairman of the HBC, Baron Strathcona and Mount Royal,[5] the *Mount Royal* was built of Douglas fir and Eastern oak at a cost of $30,000. Constructed at the Alexander Watson Shipyard in Victoria, she was designed specifically for the Skeena River. The stern-wheeler was 128-feet long and had a beam of 28 feet, "narrow enough to navigate the treacherous channels of the Skeena and large enough to house her powerful engines which, with 200 pounds pressure coursing through her 16x72-inch cylinders, turned the paddle shaft 37 times a minute, producing a speed of 12 knots with which to buck the muddy Skeena."[6] Notwithstanding her light draught—the unloaded *Mount Royal* required only 18 inches of water—she had stateroom accommodation

Although this photo of the Hazelton *is not properly identified, the vessel appears to be entering Kitselas Canyon. Two men are attaching cables to ring-bolts while three men on the forward deck by the capstan are waiting to winch the stern-wheeler upriver.*

4 Nancy Robertson, "Port Essington: Only a Dream," in *Canadian West*, Winter 1987, p. 159.
5 Port Essington *Sun*, July 20, 1907.
6 Ed Kenney, "Footnotes Along the Skeena," in *Skeena Digest*, p. 17.

for 100 passengers and cabin room for 200.[7]

The *Mount Royal* was scheduled to be launched on April 8, 1902, but because of a low tide the launch was postponed for 24 hours. At 3:50 P.M. the next day, after being christened by Thelma Thompson, the *Mount Royal* started to slide down the way—then got stuck. It took workmen two hours to get her moving again; but she was moving too slowly to steer and ran up on the bank where she remained for two days.[8]

By June the *Mount Royal* had completed trials and headed north. "Immediately, competition flared. In July, Cunningham's *Hazelton* made

7 Port Essington *Sun*, July 20, 1907.
8 Ed Kenney, *op. cit.*, p. 17.

(Right) Old trail leading to the abandoned town of Kitselas in 1992.
(Bottom) This coloured postcard view of Kitselas was probably taken c1912.

(Top) Entrance to Kitselas Canyon with the Skeena River very low in August, 1992. The sandbar and both islands seen in the photo are submerged during high water. The island protruding from the right is Ringbolt Island. (Left) The lower end of Ringbolt Island. The channel the Mount Royal attempted to use on the fateful day is on the right of the island. (Inset) One of three ringbolts still imbedded in Ringbolt Island.

The sleek Mount Royal. *Built by the HBC to stem competition from Robert Cunningham's speedy* Hazelton, *the two vessels participated in dangerous races from Port Essington to Hazelton.*

the round trip from Port Essington to Hazelton in 2 days, 7 hours, and 55 minutes. Two days later *Mount Royal* clipped 1 hour and 40 minutes from this time. Then the *Hazelton* scooted up and back in 47 hours."[9]

To outrace their competition, Captain Bonser of the *Hazelton* and Captain Johnson of the *Mount Royal* took unprecedented actions: they stole from each other's woodpiles, often ordering passengers off to help, and they sometimes steamed off with part of their cargo still on the dock. Other actions were not so amusing or innocent, however. At the end of the 1904 season, for example, Captain Johnson brought charges against Captain Bonser for, among other things, having "deliberately and with malice run his vessel into the *Mount Royal* with the purpose of injuring the latter craft."[10] Johnson also charged that Bonser had shifted a buoy placed to mark the river with the intention of causing the stranding of the *Mount Royal*.[11]

The ramming incident had occurred during the late spring of 1904. The *Hazelton* and *Mount Royal* were both at Port Essington loading up for their first trip of the season. Loaded first, the *Hazelton* churned away from the wharf unaware that the *Mount Royal* was almost ready. At Hardscrabble Rapids, about 105 miles upriver, the *Hazelton* put ashore at a wood stop to take on fuel. As this was being done, Captain Bonser sud-

9 Art Downs, *B.C.-Yukon Sternwheelers*, (Surrey: Heritage House, 1992, p. 70.
10 *Ibid*, p. 72.
11 Port Essington *Sun*, July 20, 1907.

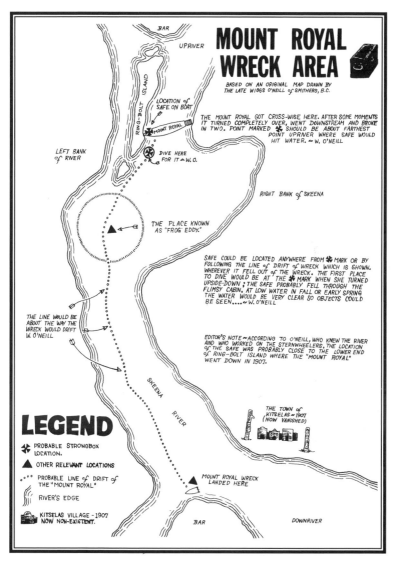

MOUNT ROYAL WRECK AREA

BASED ON AN ORIGINAL MAP DRAWN BY
THE LATE WIGGS O'NEILL of SMITHERS, B.C.

BAR

UPRIVER

RING-BOLT ISLAND

LOCATION of SAFE ON BOAT

MOUNT ROYAL

THE MOUNT ROYAL GOT CROSS-WISE HERE. AFTER SOME MOMENTS IT TURNED COMPLETELY OVER, WENT DOWNSTREAM AND BROKE IN TWO. POINT MARKED �֎ SHOULD BE ABOUT FARTHEST POINT UPRIVER WHERE SAFE WOULD HIT WATER. ~ W. O'NEILL

LEFT BANK of RIVER

DIVE HERE FOR IT ~ W. O.

RIGHT BANK of SKEENA

THE PLACE KNOWN AS "FROG EDDY."

SAFE COULD BE LOCATED ANYWHERE FROM ✖ MARK OR BY FOLLOWING THE LINE of DRIFT of WRECK WHICH IS SHOWN. WHEREVER IT FELL OUT of THE WRECK. THE FIRST PLACE TO DIVE WOULD BE AT THE ✖ MARK WHEN SHE TURNED UPSIDE-DOWN ; THE SAFE PROBABLY FELL THROUGH THE FLIMSY CABIN. AT LOW WATER IN FALL OR EARLY SPRING THE WATER WOULD BE VERY CLEAR SO OBJECTS COULD BE SEEN....~ W. O'NEILL

THE LINE WOULD BE ABOUT THE WAY THE WRECK WOULD DRIFT W. O'NEILL

EDITOR'S NOTE~ACCORDING TO O'NEILL, WHO KNEW THE RIVER AND WHO WORKED ON THE STERNWHEELERS, THE LOCATION of THE SAFE WAS PROBABLY CLOSE TO THE LOWER END of RING-BOLT ISLAND WHERE THE "MOUNT ROYAL" WENT DOWN IN 1907.

SKEENA RIVER

THE TOWN of KITSELAS ~ 1907 (NOW VANISHED)

LEGEND

✖ PROBABLE STRONGBOX LOCATION.

▲ OTHER RELEVANT LOCATIONS

∴ PROBABLE LINE of DRIFT of THE "MOUNT ROYAL"

RIVER'S EDGE

KITSELAS VILLAGE - 1907 NOW NON-EXISTENT.

MOUNT ROYAL WRECK LANDED HERE

BAR

DOWNRIVER

This map of the "Mount Royal Wreck Area" is inaccurate. The island marked as "Ringbolt Island" on the map is incorrect. The actual Ringbolt Island is located between the island named Ringbolt Island on this map and the right bank of the Skeena. See map on the following page.

denly spotted a column of smoke down river, and, with only half of the wood loaded, gave the signal to let go the lines. But before the *Hazelton* could reach top speed, the faster *Mount Royal* pulled abreast of her.

"Coming up in fairly slack water, the *Mount Royal* quickly gained and soon the vessels were bow to bow—smoke, steam and cinders belching skywards; paddlewheels frothing rapids white, passengers urging their vessels forward. Gradually *Mount Royal* thrust ahead, then suddenly was jolted as *Hazelton's* bow crushed into her starboard quarter. Fortu-

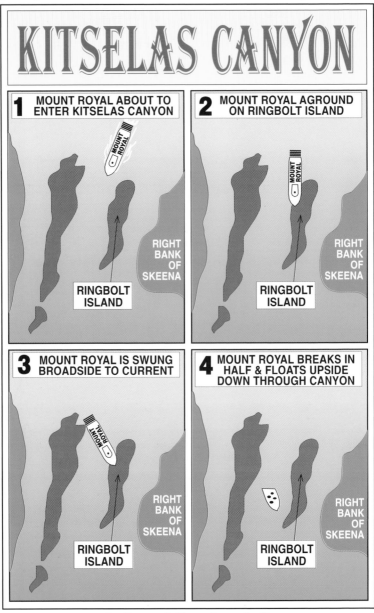

nately her overhanging main deck absorbèd the blow or the *Hazelton* could have slashed into her engine room, with deadly results.[12]

After being rammed a second time, the *Mount Royal* was forced broadside to the current, swung around and carried downstream. The *Hazelton*, meanwhile, sped upriver, her whistle tooting triumphantly.

Following this incident, both Cunningham and the HBC realized that their rivalry was not only expensive, but dangerous. It was said that the HBC paid Cunningham $2,500 to tie up the *Hazelton*, and agreed to haul his freight for free. The HBC further agreed to purchase the *Hazelton* from Cunningham if future traffic warranted, and this was in fact done. As for the *Mount Royal,* she was wrecked in Kitselas Canyon in 1907 with the loss of six men and, according to legend, a fortune in gold.

At 9 A.M. on that fateful Saturday, July 6, 1907, the *Mount Royal* pulled away from the *Hazelton* wharf and headed down river for Port

12 Art Downs, *op. cit.*, p. 72.

(Left) The stern-wheeler Hazelton at old Hazelton in 1992. (Below) The Skeena River at Old Hazelton. At 9 a.m. on Saturday, July 6, 1907, the Mount Royal set out from here on her final ill-fated journey.

Essington. Aboard the vessel were 22 crew members and 27 passengers. Most of the passengers were Indians bound for the fishing grounds, but there were a number of whites as well: M. Rhodes had spent a year in the Twelka country, while Mrs. F.M. Phillips was en route from Hazelton to her home in The Dalles, Oregon. Other passengers included E.E. Potts of Vancouver, K.H. Rolley of Matsqui and O. Spidal of Camrose, Alberta.[13]

The voyage down river was uneventful until they reached the mouth of Kitselas Canyon, "600 yards of the roughest navigable water in the world."[14] It was 3:04 P.M. when the *Mount Royal* reached the entrance to the canyon: 11 minutes later she "was going through the awful canyon in tatters, bottom up and unpiloted—a coffin for six of her crew."[15]

The first report on the incident that appeared in the Port Essington Sun the same day painted a rather grim picture. "She carried a good passenger list and few are believed to have been saved." Three days later an inquest was held into the tragedy, and through it the details of just what happened began to emerge.

According to the testimony of Joseph Offett, a crewman, the river was extremely high at the time and a strong wind was blowing. As they approached the canyon, Captain Johnson gave the usual order to "stand with fenders." The *Mount Royal* was just entering the canyon when "a gust sent the boat crossways, held her in that position for a few minutes and drove her nose five feet up Ringbolt island, a small island at the entrance, coming down."[16]

Ringbolt Island was so named because ringbolts were embedded into the rock to enable stern-wheelers to winch themselves through the canyon against the strong current. Three ringbolts are still visible on the rocky island today. On page 115 you will see a map entitled the "Mount Royal Wreck Area."[17] This map, however, is inaccurate. First, the island identified as "Ringbolt Island" is incorrect. There are two islands at the mouth of Kitselas Canyon (See map entitled Kitselas Canyon). When I visited the area in the summer of 1992, the water of the Skeena River was low and it was possible to walk across to the first island, not shown on Barlee's map, which is in fact Ringbolt Island. During extremely high water, the Skeena flows between the shore and the first island (Ringbolt), as it did at the time of the tragedy in 1907.

The gap between the shore and Ringbolt Island is extremely narrow in places and walking through it at low water it is difficult to believe that stern-wheelers could actually pass through it. However, in high water, the gap is widened by the sloping cliffs, and this was in fact one of the preferred routes through the canyon. Between Ringbolt Island and the

13 Port Essington *Sun*, July 13, 1907.
14 *Ibid.*
15 *Ibid.*
16 *Ibid.*
17 Drawn by N.L. Barlee, this map first appeared in *Canada West*, in the Spring, 1972 issue. It later was reproduced in *The Best of Canada West*, (Langley: Stagecoach Publishing, 1978, p. 73.)

larger island, identified incorrectly as Ringbolt Island on Barlee's map, is another narrow passageway, although much wider that the one between the shore and Ringbolt Island. It is uncertain by the testimony which passageway Johnson had selected on that fateful day. Similarly, the reports do not state in which direction the vessel was pushed by the gust of wind, left or right: but my research indicates that he was attempting to pass between Ringbolt Island and the larger island.

Once the *Mount Royal* was grounded on Ringbolt Island, Captain Johnson ordered everyone ashore. All the passengers and most of the crew crossed over a gangplank to Ringbolt Island, where they got an excellent view of the ensuing tragedy. Johnson, who according to testimony remained calm and collected, then instructed crewmen to attach a cable to the bolts on Ringbolt Island to securely fasten the vessel. Unfortunately, the capstan had been damaged by the collision with the island and was not functioning. W.L. Lewis, the first officer, then ordered a cable to be attached to the "after cleat" in another attempt secure the vessel. The thinking was that if the stern could be kept from swinging across the river, the *Mount Royal* might yet be saved. But it was too late.

E. Harrison Bessett, watching from Ringbolt Island, described what happened next.

"The officers and crew were working with the boat to get it free from the island. They got a cable out but the capstan would not work. The stern of the boat swung around and caught on the opposite side of the channel. The passengers were all on shore. The boat listed and tipped over and took in a good deal of water. The captain came out from the wheel house, looked at the boat and shouted, 'All ashore.' The boat then began to turn over. The captain jumped down the companion way, then to the lower deck and on to the rocks as the boat was turning over. Saw the boat bottom up with four men on it. Heard noise of explosion of boiler. The (wheel) house on the boat was broken off and the lower bow was broken off also ten or fifteen feet in length from the end of the boat. These four men were afterwards rescued."[18] Six other crewmen, first officer W.L. Lewis, purser James O'Keefe, steward Archie Willis, fireman Bert Frayne, carpenter Jero Morishima and deck boy Frank Ancante, were not as fortunate.

Offett testified that he and Willis were working on the cable when they were ordered ashore. However, the *Mount Royal* flipped over so quickly that neither had a chance to escape. Offett was fortunate enough to catch the rim of a life boat and scramble on to the bottom of the overturned stern-wheeler. He was one of the four men rescued by residents of Kitselas, just below the canyon. Willis was trapped in the wreckage and drowned, his body being the only one recovered that day.

On Sunday, September 21, 1907, the Port Essington *Sun* reported that the remains of James O'Keefe was found by two Indians near Trout

18 Port Essington *Sun*, July 13, 1907.

Creek. The 20-year-old O'Keefe, a resident of Victoria, was born in Halifax, Nova Scotia. He was serving in his second year aboard the *Mount Royal* when the accident occurred. On October 5 the *Sun* reported that another body had been found. At first it was thought that the badly decomposed body was the remains of Bert Frayne, the fireman. However, identification marks found on the clothing proved that it was in fact the Japanese carpenter Jero Morishima. It is not known if the

(Above) The narrow gap between Ringbolt Island and the right bank of the Skeena River is dry during low water.
(Below) The Mount Royal *docked on the Skeena River. Although the location is not specified, it appears to be opposite Port Essington.*

remaining bodies were ever found.

Which brings us to the all important question—what about the alleged treasure? "Since that disastrous day, July 6, 1907," wrote N.L. Barlee, "the *Mount Royal* has been the subject of much speculation. It was known that the strongbox on board the ship was lost at the time of the sinking and has never been recovered. Although there is considerable controversy concerning the contents of the safe—with estimates ranging as high as $40,000 to as low as $700—the actual amount in cash probably approached the latter figure."[19]

Charlie Durham, a resident of Usk, was at Kitselas in 1907 when the overturned bow of the *Mount Royal* drifted down river with its four occupants. Durham, who participated in the rescue and helped to remove survivors from Ringbolt Island, died in 1958 at the age of 97. Four years prior to his death he was interviewed by Rita Mary Rogerson regarding the *Mount Royal* tragedy. In a subsequent article written for *B.C. Digest*, Rogerson quotes Durham. "The *Mount Royal* was loaded with furs, bales were lashed to her outside railing. The Indians picked up quite a bit and had it drying at New Town. The safe fell out when the boat turned over and rumor had it that there was $100,000 in gold in the safe."

---

19 N.L. Barlee, *The Best of Canada West*, (Langley: Stagecoach publing, 1978, p. 74.

This photograph, taken in 1962, shows William Dunn standing beside the remains of the Mount Royal's *paddlewheel. It had been dug from Kitselas Canyon by the owner of the Kitselas Motel.*

But when Rogerson asked Charlie directly if he thought there actually was gold in the safe, he replied: "No. If there was the Hudson's Bay Company would have been after it years ago."

Another reference to the treasure was written by Dr. R.G. Large in *Skeena: River of Destiny.* According to Large, on that fateful trip the *Mount Royal* "was descending the river with a load of passengers and thirty thousand dollars in gold dust."

So who is right and who is wrong? Well, since I do not have the *Mount Royal's* manifest for that final voyage, I must rely on whatever firsthand accounts that are available. One of the best sources of information are the newspapers of the day.

Six days after the tragedy, on Sunday, July 13, the Port Essington *Sun* reported that: "Two tons of furs were on the *Royal* when she went down." In the same issue the newspaper mentioned that a passenger named M. Rhodes had lost a "sum of money, records and maps of the Twelka country," which had been wrapped up in his blankets at the time of the mishap.

Two weeks later the same newspaper stated: "Among the fur losses by the *Mt. Royal* wreck are R.S. Sargent, of Hazelton, who was shipping out $800 worth of skins; R. Cunningham & Sons, Ltd. $1,000; and Alex Oaks, $750. Hopes are entertained that a good many of these skins will yet be recovered, as they were packed in boxes, and in all likelihood drifted ashore."

Nowhere in the *Sun's* reporting of the original tragedy and subsequent accounts is there any mention of the *Mount Royal's* safe or a treasure—of any amount. It seems hardly conceivable to me that the newspaper would omit to mention a treasure in gold, if it existed, while mentioning a small sum of money lost by a passenger and twice mentioning the furs that were aboard. Based on this, and the lack of clear evidence to the contrary, I must hold the opinion that no treasure worth salvaging remains at the bottom of Kitselas Canyon. But treasure stories being what they are, the rumours of a golden treasure will probably persist for many years to come.   ❀

CHAPTER 10

THE TREASURE OF
THE SS PACIFIC

*The Pacific sailed out of Victoria on November 4, 1875 crammed with
freight and bulging with over 275 passengers and crew. She also carried
$100,000 in gold. Later that night the Pacific and her golden treasure lay
on the bottom of the ocean. There were only two survivors.*

BUILT in 1851, the *Pacific* began her career by transporting passengers between Panama and San Francisco. During the Fraser River
gold rush, the 900-ton sidewheel steamer brought miners up
from California. In the early 1860s she ran aground and was severely
damaged, but was patched up and put back into service. From 1872 to
1875 the *Pacific* was retired from active service; but the start of a new
gold rush in the Cassiar district resulted in her being put back into
service on the Victoria-Puget Sound-San Francisco run. Throughout her
career the ship had seldom been inspected by any government official,
and then only in the most casual or superficial way.

How many passengers she carried on her last fateful voyage will
never be known, since many tickets were sold at the last minute. The fare
was only $5, as the owners of the *Pacific* were engaged in a price war
with a rival firm, the Pacific Mail and Steamship Company. Sometimes
these companies even allowed passengers to travel free, merely in order
to take business from their rival. As well, since children paid no fare, it is
possible that there were many more on board than the later official estimate of about 275.

Jefferson D. Howell, captain of the *Pacific* had the unusual distinc-
tion of being a brother-in-law of Jefferson Davis, first and only president
of the Confederate states in the recent Civil War. Howell had been an
officer in the Confederate Navy until the defeat of the south, when he
had come west to start life anew.

The arrival of the *Pacific* in Victoria late in October 1875 attracted little attention. The general public was more interested in various signs of
reviving prosperity. On November 4, 1875, she began taking on passengers for a scheduled run to San Francisco. Some of those who boarded,
like Sewell P. Moody, were men who had business connections in California. On the other hand, J.H. Sullivan, Gold Commissioner of the Cas-

JEFFERSON D. HOWELL
CAPTAIN

NEIL HENLEY
SURVIVOR

F.H. JELLY
SURVIVOR

siar district, was on route to a well-earned holiday in Ireland. Capt. Otis Parsons had sold his interest in some Fraser River steamers for $40,000 in gold, and was on his way to San Francisco with his family to spend part of it. The *Pacific's* cargo was mostly coal and potatoes and, according to D.W. Higgins, editor of the *Colonist*, who saw her just before she sailed, the ship was "loaded to the gunwhale with freight, and so filled with passengers that all the berth room was occupied, and the saloons and decks were utilized as sleeping spaces." Also on board was nearly $100,000 in gold dust and bullion.

Shortly after the *Pacific* left Victoria on Thursday, November 4, 1875, it was noticed that she was listing badly. To remedy the situation, the lifeboats on one side of the ship were filled with water! Later, when that side of the vessel seemed too low, those lifeboats were emptied and some on the other side were filled. Under such circumstances and direction, the *Pacific* made her way through the Strait of Juan de Fuca and around Cape Flattery at its entrance.

By 8 P.M. that night, the *Pacific* was 40 miles south of the Cape. As it was late in the year, most of her passengers had retired for the night. Outside the sky was clear and, although the wind was brisk, the sea was comparatively smooth. Suddenly there was a violent jar, which made the ship shudder. Some passengers, awakened by the commotion, hastily dressed and went on deck. Here they were told that the *Pacific* had collided with another vessel, but that there was no immediate danger.

The lights of the other ship (later identified as the sailing vessel *Orpheus*) could be seen receding in the distance, and some passengers returned to bed. They quickly realized, however, that something was seriously wrong, and once more rushed on deck. This time they found a scene of complete confusion. It was obvious that the *Pacific* was sinking, and efforts were being made to launch the boats. However, no boat drill

Two coloured postcards of Victoria. The one above shows the Canadian Pacific Railway docks, while the one below is a view of Government Street. Neither postcard is dated.

had been held, and neither passengers nor crew knew what to do. Moreover, the mechanism which released the boats was jammed from long disuse. Adding to the turmoil was the fact that some of the boats were still full of water, while others had no oars in them. To further compound the situation, the ship's lights had gone out. Nevertheless, by cutting their lashings with axes, the crew managed to launch a few boats.

Disorder reigned. A group of women were herded into one boat, and several of the crew promptly got in beside them. When they were criticized for this, they replied that they were there to look after the ladies. A male passenger who had entered the boat with his wife was promptly ejected, despite her tearful pleas.

The ship settled fast, breaking in two just before she disappeared. Three hundred people struggled in the cold water, seeking pieces of wreckage to which they could cling. Most of the women quickly disappeared, as the voluminous clothing of the time absorbed large quantities of water. In retrospect, it appears that at least 20 people survived the initial sinking and managed to keep afloat by clinging to large pieces of wreckage. However, all but two of these were eventually benumbed by the cold and washed away.

One of the two survivors was a young man from Port Stanley, Ontario, named Henry Jelley. He had been engaged on the Canadian Pacific Railway survey, and was on his way back to eastern Canada by way of the American transcontinental railway, in operation since 1869. Seeing the wheelhouse floating in the water with a single man clinging to it, he made his way to it and soon the two were drifting slowly up the Pacific coast toward Cape Flattery. Jelley's companion proved to be a young man from Maine who had done very well in the Cariboo and was now on his way home.

The two men survived the night, but, at 4 o'clock the next afternoon, Jelley's companion became delirious. Finally he lay back and quietly died. The two men had tied themselves to their raft, and Jelley now cut his companion loose.

By early Saturday morning the mountains of Vancouver Island loomed up, and Jelley had hopes that before long he would be washed ashore on its desolate coast. When he was only three miles from the island, a ship came in view which proved to be the American bark *Messenger*. Jelley was able to attract the attention of those on board, and at 10 o'clock on Saturday morning he was rescued and brought to Port Townsend, from where he made his way to Victoria.

Jelley later testified that the ship was already listing when she left Victoria, probably because her cargo was poorly stowed. He confirmed that he "saw water put in the boats between Victoria and Race Rocks" and that "there were oars in the two large boats but the two forward boats had no oars in them." He estimated that the five boats carried by the ship would hold a total of 145 people. This prompted the foreman of the coroner's jury to point out that "At least 155 persons would have had to stay and drown if the boats had got away." Jelley also said that the mechanism for launching the boats was complicated and proved hard to operate.

There had been but one other survivor, a member of the crew. He was a native of the Hebrides named Neil Henley, who was picked up by the United States revenue cutter *Oliver Wolcott*. Henley also testified that he had "seen water put in those boats to trim ship" and gave a vivid account of the last quarter hour of the *Pacific*:

"The wind was freshening from the southward when I went to bed. It was pretty dark. Saw a few passengers about the pilot-house at 8 o'clock; the weather was not thick or foggy; saw no lights. The sea was not rough. I went at once to my bunk when relieved, stripped off, and fell asleep.

"The first I heard afterwards was a crash; my bunk was forward of the steerage. The steerage was above us on the 'tween deck. I was below the 'tween deck on the starboard side. I was sleeping pretty near on a level with the water; I woke up with the crash. I heard and saw the water coming in through the bows. There was no bulkhead between me and the stern of the ship. I didn't look for the planks having parted; the water came in with a rush—flying in. There was water on the floor of the fore-castle when I turned out. I put on a jacket and ran up the companion-way."

Henley confirmed that there was little sign of the captain, or indeed of any sort of organized direction. He personally had to replace the plug in the bottom of one boat, without which it would have been useless:

"The first thing I did was to put the plug in the boat, which was not in when I got there; can give no reason why the plug was not in. After the boats were washed out, the officer of the watch should have seen that the plugs were put in.

"The boat tackle was loosened when I looked. I got hold of the line and tried to raise her. The blocks were hooked on the boat. No one seemed to be in command giving direction.

"We could not raise the boat because it was full of people. Don't know whether it was full when I got in to put the plug in. Tried to get the people out. Some would come out and then go back again. Don't think there were any women in this boat. Forget if there were any of the crew in it. Don't remember if there were any of the crew helping me to raise the boat.

"I left this boat and went to the port boat which I saw ladies in. Saw the purser and the chief engineer there. The stern of the boat was raised by men pulling at the rope. The davit was not swung out over the ship. Cannot tell how many ladies were in the boat. There were lights there. The boat was not lowered. It was left there so that when the ship sank it would float off. The chief engineer suggested this.

"The fires were out by this time, and the engines had stopped, but it was feared the boat would be stove on account of the heavy swell. Forget if there were children in the boat. Shortly after this the boat floated off, the water being close to the hurricane deck, and the ship going down fast.

Prospectors in Northern British Columbia. When the Cassiar gold rush began, the ill-fated sidewheel steamer the Ss Pacific, below, was again pressed into service.

"The chief engineer was standing in the stern of the boat, and I was alongside of him. The line was fast, and the fall was cut when the water came under the boat. The chief engineer had an axe in his hand to cut the line. It was not long that we had to wait for the water to reach the boat. Saw the stern fall cut by the chief engineer. Don't know who cut the bow fall. We floated off from the ship and were thrown back against the ship by the swell. There was a crowd of men around the boat trying to get in.

"We might have got a boat's length from the ship, but the boat was so crammed with people she could not be rowed. Think the boat was damaged by coming against the ship, as I found she was half full of water immediately afterward, and I sprang into the water. This was the last I saw of the boat."

Henley had managed to climb on board a large piece of wreckage, where he found the captain, three members of the crew and three passengers, including a woman. One by one the others had succumbed, and Henley drifted, alone and helpless, until he was picked by the *Oliver Wolcott*, after having been in the water from Thursday night till Monday morning.

Testimony was also given by some members of the crew of the *Orpheus*. It appeared that one reason for the collision was that the captain of the *Orpheus* had been uncertain of his ship's location and had hoped to obtain it from the *Pacific*. To do this he had brought his ship very close to the steamer, where an error of judgement on someone's part had resulted in the *Pacific* striking the *Orpheus* and losing some of her rigging. At first Captain Sawyer had feared that the *Orpheus* was in danger of sinking, but when a quick examination had showed that she was not taking water, he had sailed away without waiting to inquire if the *Pacific* was in need of help. This in itself contributed greatly to the loss of life. As one crewman of the *Orpheus* declared at the Victoria inquest:

"If the ship had hove to immediately, witness thought most of the people on the steamer might have been saved, and at all events those on the raft might have been rescued, as the boat could have picked them up."

The *Orpheus* herself, a ship of 1,100 tons, en route from San Francisco to Nanaimo to load coal, had eventually run ashore in Barkley Sound, apparently because her captain had confused the comparatively new light on Cape Beale at its entrance with that on Cape Flattery. This cast some doubt on his competence (and later resulted in an American inquiry into his conduct). Meanwhile testimony by other members of his crew did little to enhance his reputation:

"Had not seen the captain drinking; could not tell by his manner whether he was drunk or sober. The captain was one of the worst men witness had ever sailed with. Did not hoist any signal of distress.

"I thought something must be wrong with the steamer and reported so to the captain.

"The officers drank as much as they could get hold of. There was plenty of liquor after the ship went ashore, but could not say if they could get at it while she was afloat."

Another member of the *Orpheus'* crew agreed that "the captain drank pretty hard sometimes."

The inquest soon focused attention on the *Pacific's* seaworthiness. The ship was about 25 years old and had passed through numerous hands before being bought with five others for the total sum of $230,000—an indication that none of them were considered very valuable.

The *Colonist* undoubtedly spoke for the whole community when it declared:

"We can call to mind no more appalling instance of a wanton waste of human life than this calamity presents. The evidence taken before the coroner's jury as to the unseaworthiness of the steamer leads irresistibly to the conclusion that had she not collided with the *Orpheus* she must soon have fallen to pieces from a sheer inability to hold together. One skilled witness swore that 'her timbers could be shovelled out of her.'

"To sum up, these points present themselves to the writer. First, that the *Pacific* was rotten and unseaworthy, and known to be such by her owners. Second, that she was not properly equipped for a voyage to sea. Third, that twice as many passengers were taken as she had boat accommodation for. Fourth, that none of her officers were to be relied on in an emergency. Fifth, that her crew were weak, inefficient and overworked. Sixth, that the watch on deck at the time of the collision was insufficient. Seventh, that censurable as the *Orpheus* clearly was, the disaster was avoidable by the exercise of ordinary care on the part of the steamship."

Captain Sawyer had his own version of the collision with the *Pacific*:

"When, after I found I was not seriously damaged, I looked for the steamer, I just saw a light on our starboard quarter, and when I looked again it was gone. There has been a great deal said about the crying and screaming of the women and children on the steamer. Not one sound was heard from her by any one on my ship, neither was anyone seen on board of her. Neither did anyone on my ship think for a moment that any injury of any kind had happened to the steamer, for at 1:30 that night as the sailors were furling the spanker, they commenced to growl, as sailors will, about the steamer, after running us down, to go off and leave us in that shape, without stopping to inquire whether we were injured or not."

The captain's testimony was not, however, supported by his crew:

"The sailors on the *Orpheus* afterwards testified that they begged Captain Sawyer to bring his ship round and lower a boat and attempt to save some of the drowning passengers. He would not listen to their appeals but headed his vessel toward the Vancouver (sic) shore, and ran her on the beach."

The American board investigating the loss of the *Orpheus*, meeting behind closed doors, eventually exonerated her captain, blaming instead poor steering by his officers. It found no fault attaching to Captain Sawyer for the loss of the *Pacific* either, declaring (in apparent contradiction to Sawyer's own testimony that he had seen no one on board her) that "it was impossible to take steps for the preservation of life after the collision on account of the panic among the passengers."

Despite his acquittal, Captain Sawyer soon afterwards retired from the sea, living out his days at Port Townsend, where he died in 1894.

The *Colonist* unhesitatingly called the American inquiry a complete whitewash. It noted that as both ships were American, they were not subject to Canadian inspection, but the paper recommended that use should be made of the Canadian regulation by which the Postmaster-General had the right to inspect any ship seeking a contract to carry mail. It also urged the signing of an international agreement covering all matters connected with the safety of ships on the Pacific coast.

Over a century has passed since the tragedy of the *Pacific*. Since the sinking is well documented, we need concern ourselves only with her treasure. Although specific figures are impossible to ascertain, the existence of a large treasure is undisputed. F.W. Howay, in his *British Columbia Historical*, states that the Pacific "steamed out of Victoria Harbour on her last trip, carrying about $100,000 in treasure."

Capt. Otis Parsons, one of the victims in the tragedy, had himself taken aboard $40,000.

It's possible, in fact, that her treasure could have been considerably higher, since it is uncertain if this $100,000 figure includes the $40,000 owned by Captain Parsons. Similarly, the ship was loaded with numerous prospectors, many of whom undoubtedly possessed their own treasure of varying sizes. As this earlier item, which appeared in the November 18, 1861 issue of the *Colonist*, would tend to indicate, that is a very real possibility:

"DEPARTURE OF THE *PACIFIC*.—The steamship *Pacific* went to sea yesterday morning, from Esquimalt, at 9 o'clock. She had on board nearly 200 miners and others as passengers from this place, and 120 United States soldiers from the Sound. Wells, Fargo, and Co. shipped 205,998 dollars in gold dust. The total shipment, including the amounts in private hands, will reach 400,000 dollars (£80,000)."

However, even if the amount aboard the *Pacific* when she foundered in 1875 was only $100,000, it should be sufficient to satisfy any treasure seeker, for, at today's prices, $100,000 worth of gold dust and bullion would be worth nearly $3 million. Alas, even though it is an enticing treasure, the mere fact that it lies in part of a shipwreck takes it out of the hands of most treasure enthusiasts. Those individuals will have to content themselves with wishful thinking as they visualize the treasure of the Pacific which lies in only 12 or 13 fathoms of water off Cape Flattery.

CHAPTER 11

BROTHER XII'S
MISSING GOLD

With a blend of black magic, occultism, sex and lost gold, the weird but fascinating story of Brother Twelve seems too incredible to be true. But the hundreds of bilked disciples who had placed their faith and their funds under his care found out that Brother Twelve was all too real.

EDWARD Arthur Wilson was born in Birmingham, England, on July 25, 1878. Edward and his two sisters were raised by their parents, Thomas Wilson and Sarah Pearsall, in an atmosphere of strict religious devotion. Young Edward was also influenced by the sea. As a boy he apprenticed on a Royal Navy windjammer, acquiring skills through which he earned his living for most of his life. On some of his early voyages Edward helped transport kidnapped Negroes from Africa to Turkey, where they were sold as slaves. In 1902, the 24-year-old Wilson arrived in New Zealand, where he met and married Margery Clark. The marriage was blessed with a son and daughter, which Wilson supported by working as a draftsman, surveyor, electrician and farmer.[1]

But the globe-travelling Wilson soon grew restless, and in 1907 he brought his family to Victoria where he gained employment as a baggage clerk for the Dominion Express Company. Although promoted several times, Wilson quit when he was denied a raise in pay. He then went to work as a pilot on lumber schooners and coastal steamers plying between San Francisco and Alaska. This new employment kept Wilson away from home for long periods of time, and in 1912 he abandoned his wife and children. Destitute, they eventually returned to New Zealand.

Wilson next headed for the Orient, and from 1912 to 1924 he travelled around the world. In the fall of 1924, the 46-year-old Wilson, nearly destitute and in failing health, arrived in a small village in southern France. "A slender man with delicate features, iron-grey hair, and a neatly

EDWARD ARTHUR WILSON
A.K.A. BROTHER TWELVE

---

1 John Oliphant, *Brother Twelve*, (Toronto: McClelland & Stewart, 1991, pp. 17-19.)

trimmed Van Dyke beard,"[2] Wilson's travels had taken him to shrines and temples in Egypt, India, China and Mexico. "He studied the religions of the world, investigated numerous occult doctrines, and immersed himself in the teachings of Theosophy."[3]

On October 19, 1924, Wilson was not feeling well and retired early. However, when he lit the bedside candle, Wilson saw a vision of the Tau Cross, more commonly known as the ankh or Egyptian ansate cross, suspended in mid-air. Three days later, having again gone to bed early, Wilson revealed that a voice, which he claimed belonged to a powerful Egyptian deity, spoke to him. These two incidents were to dramatically alter the course of Wilson's life. By February, 1926, Wilson had completed the manuscript of the book *The Three Truths*, the material for which, according to Wilson, had been dictated to him while he was in a trance by the Master of Wisdom. The Master also informed Wilson that he had been "chosen to be his personal chela or disciple. Since the Master was the Twelfth Brother in the Great White Lodge, he gave Wilson, as his disciple, the name 'Brother Twelve,' also written, according to occult convention, with the Roman numerals 'XII'."[4]

In May Wilson went to England, where he was already being hailed as a "gifted psychic and major profit." It was here that his new movement, the Aquarian Foundation, was formed. Wilson's efforts in occult circles garnered enthusiastic support, and by January, 1927, he advised Foundation members that he had been directed by the Master to inaugurate the work of the White Lodge in North America.

In early March Wilson was well received by Theosophical Society members in Montreal, followed by another enthusiastic crowd in Ottawa 10 days later. Following his tremendously successful eastern swing, which also included speeches to Theosophical Lodges in Toronto, Hamilton, London and Windsor, Wilson boarded the train for British Columbia. From Vancouver, he took the *Princess Louise* to Nanaimo, where he rented a house in nearby Northfield. A few days later Wilson contacted a Vancouver lawyer named Edward Lucas who had written to him in England. The two men met for the first time at Nanaimo on March 13. A week later, Wilson travelled to Lucas' Vancouver home.

The late Gwen Cash, Canada's first woman reporter, wrote a chapter on Brother Twelve in her book *Off The Record*. Cash, who first learned of him through Lucas, also had the opportunity to interview Phil Fisher and Robert England, both of whom were part of Brother Twelve's inner circle and well acquainted with the Foundation's activities.

According to Cash, Edward Lucas, who sympathized with Brother Twelve's ideals, helped him to locate at Cedar, on the Vancouver Island seashore, 10 miles south of Nanaimo. Lucas drew up a charter for the

2 *Ibid*, p. 9
3 *Ibid*.
4 *Ibid*, p. 13.

Brother Twelve and the governors of the Aquarian Foundation at their first general meeting, July 25, 1927. Left to right: Edward Lucas (back to camera), Joseph Benner, Maurice Von Platen, Edward Wilson, Phillip Fisher, Will Comfort and Coulson Turnbull.

Aquarian Foundation, which was so named because, according to theosophical mysticism, the Pisces age had ended and the Aquarian age had begun.

"Some 2,500 Seekers were enroled at Cedar by the Sea. Some of them were pretty important people; like Will Levington Comfort, a *Saturday Evening Post* writer; occultist Sir Kenneth MacKenzie of Turnbridge Wells, England; Maurice von Platten, millionaire organ builder of Chicago; Joseph Benner, publisher of *The Sun*, Akron, Ohio; and George Hubbard, Toronto newsman. Money rolled in. Some of the Seekers built houses at Cedar. Others just camped there during summers."[5]

The Aquarian Foundation included a board of governors composed of Wilson and six highly reputable men; Will Comfort, Coulson Turnbull, Maurice Von Platen, Joseph Benner, Edward Lucas and Phillip Fisher. At first, everything appeared to be above board, as earnest groups of men and women studied occultism and engaged in debates. However, when the first issue of the Foundation's monthly magazine, *The Chalice*, was published in November, 1927, some members realized that the Foundation was really a militant political organization. In the ensuing months Brother Twelve laid plans to start a third political party in the United States. He also attempted to start a political organization in England.

In 1928 Brother Twelve purchased 400 acres on nearby Valdes Island where he planned to build a separate community for selected disciples at what he called the Mandieh Settlement. That July, while taking a train from Seattle to Chicago, Brother Twelve met Mrs. Myrtle Baumgartner. After some casual conversation, the two soon retired to Brother Twelve's sleeper. When Brother Twelve returned to Cedar in August, Myrtle,

5 Gwen Cash, *Off The Record*, (Langley: Stagecoach Publishing, 1977, p. 143.)

already pregnant, returned with him. In an attempt to keep his illicit love affair a secret, Brother Twelve immediately placed Myrtle in a cabin on Valdes Island.

Despite the precautions, however, word soon leaked out that Wilson had taken a mistress. The upset disciples demanded an explanation. Their concerns escalated to outrage and revolt when Brother Twelve brought Myrtle back to Cedar and desecrated the secret retreat called the House of Mystery by having sex with her there. But illicit sex was not Wilson's only indiscretion. He became secretive about Valdes Island and carried out his plans in the dark of night without the knowledge or approval of the governors.

Matters finally came to a head at a meeting held on September 18 when the governors demanded Wilson explain his radical behaviour and love affair with Mrytle. Maurice Von Platen insisted that Wilson surrender control of the Foundation or agree to dissolve it. At first Wilson refused and adjourned the meeting. Later, after a conversation with Lucas, Wilson reconsidered, and that afternoon he informed Von Platen, Robert DeLuce and Coulson Turnbull that their membership had been cancelled. Another governor, Phil Fisher, had resigned 10 days earlier.

On October 24, the three dissenting governors, carrying the proxy for a fourth, attended a general meeting that was expected to be a formality in the dissolving of the Aquarian Foundation. Wilson, however, had other plans. Empowered by the society's bylaws to increase the number of governors to 12, he had appointed Alfred and Annie Barley and George and Louise Hobart as new governors. This gave Wilson a majority of five votes to four, and when the motion to dissolve the Foundation was presented, it was defeated.

Although out maneuvered, the dissenting governors were not about to give up. They left Cedar and drove immediately to the Nanaimo police station where they charged Wilson with misappropriating $13,000 from the Aquarian Foundation. Later that day Wilson was arrested and taken to the Nanaimo courthouse.

At the preliminary trial, held on October 30 before a packed courtroom, Robert England, the Foundation's secretary-treasurer, testified that Wilson had received a cheque of $23,000 from Mary Connally. However, instead of depositing it all into the account of the Aquarian Foundation, Wilson had instructed him to put $8,000 into the account of the Mandieh Settlement Fund and $5,000 into Wilson's personal account.

Prosecutor T.P. Morton elicited from England the fact that the deed to the Mandieh Settlement on Valdes Island was made out in the name of Wilson and not the Aquarian Foundation. But when Mary Connally appeared in court, she testified that her donation had been made to Wilson personally, not the Aquarian Foundation, and he was free to dispose of the funds as he saw fit. Despite this disclosure, Judge Beevor-Potts bound Wilson over on a $5,000 bond to appear at the fall assizes.

When the fall assizes opened on November 20 before another packed courtroom, Robert England, the prosecutor's star witness, failed to appear. Many believed that England, who was himself on trial for having stolen $2,800 in Aquarian funds, had simply run off with the money. Others, however, felt he had been the victim of foul play.

England, who had been sent to Seattle by Lucas to retrieve the $2,800 from a safety deposit box, was last seen at a Seattle bus station by Nellie Little. A young woman whose family owned a general store at Cedar, Nellie saw the $2,800 in England's possession. After boarding the bus for the journey north, England, who claimed that he was being followed, was never seen or heard from again. Meanwhile, the jury returned verdicts of "no true bill" against both England and Wilson.

Despite Wilson's victory, the B.C. government met on December 12 to hear the application from the dissenting governors on whether or not to dissolve the Aquarian Foundation. After hearing testimony from both sides, the government said it would give its decision at a later date.

During the first three months of 1929, while he awaited the government's decision, Wilson continued to build the Mandieh Settlement on Valdes Island. In April, after taking Mary Connally on a tour of Valdes, Wilson pointed out two islands, DeCourcy and Ruxton, which he said were crucial to his future plans. Connally promptly acquired the two islands for him.

Meanwhile, members who had remained loyal to Brother Twelve began to move from Cedar to the Mandieh Settlement, or as it now became known, the Brother's Centre. During this time new members of the colony continued to arrive, selling their worldly possessions and giving the proceeds to Wilson. It was during this time also that Mabel Skottowe, better known as the infamous Madame Zee, entered Wilson's life.

Skottowe had been a loyal follower of Brother Twelve for years. In Florida she met Roger Painter, the "Poultry King," and the two became romantically involved. In 1927 they became secretaries of the Aquarian Foundation of Florida. Painter had frequently made donations of $5,000 and $10,000 to Brother Twelve, and in 1929 he and Mabel received an invitation to join Wilson on Valdes Island. Turning his million dollar poultry business over to his brother, Painter headed north with $90,000 in cash for Wilson.

Although Skottowe and Painter were lovers, she and Wilson were soon attracted to each other and began to spend a lot of time together. Skottowe stayed in a tent in the bush, to which Wilson became a frequent late night visitor. One morning after Painter, jealous with rage, brutally

ROGER PAINTER

beat Mabel, Wilson banished him from the island. Elma Wilson, although not legally married to Wilson, had been his loyal mate from the early days in the south seas when he had taken seriously ill and she had nursed him back to health. His constant companion ever since, she was devastated by the love affair between Brother Twelve and Madame Zee. Wilson, however, displayed no remorse or guilt, and soon Madam Zee moved in with him. In addition to being his lover, Madame Zee became Wilson's personal secretary and assisted him in the day-to-day running of the colony.

"The disciples soon discovered that Madame Zee, a tireless worker herself, was a harsh task-mistress. She was impatient, short-tempered, and carried a riding crop or quirt, which she didn't hesitate to use when her temper got the better of her."[6]

In the fall of 1929 Wilson began to turn DeCourcy Island into the new centre of his activities, and at the end of September he and Madame Zee moved into the new house that had been built at the south end of the island. This move essentially secluded Brother Twelve from his disciples.

For nearly a year the B.C. government had delayed its decision on the Aquarian Foundation in the hopes that the two factions could resolve their differences. The bitterness between the two groups made this impossible, however, so on November 15, 1929, the cabinet passed an Order-In-Council dissolving the society. Although each landowner at Cedar was given title to his property, Wilson was pleased with the results, since it did not interfere with his operations on Valdes and DeCourcy islands. However, he was now forbidden by law from using the name Aquarian Foundation.

Three weeks later Brother Twelve surprised his disciples by announcing that he and Madame Zee were going to England on important matters. While there he purchased a sturdy, 62-foot Brixham trawler which he rechristened the *Lady Royal*. In March they put to sea with a local sailor for the return trip to British Columbia. After a circuitous route, the vessel arrived at DeCourcy Island on November 6, 11 months after their departure.

For some time after their return, Brother Twelve and Madame Zee subjected their disciples to hard physical labour and terrible living conditions. Even Mary Connally, who had been one of Wilson's staunchest supporters, both vocally and financially, was not spared. At one point she lost 28 pounds working the fields, and there were rumours that the frail, elderly woman had even been yoked to a plow.

During this time Wilson shared his bed with other women, and sex between his older disciples and some of the younger female colonists was apparently condoned and even encouraged. In March, 1931, Wilson changed his name to Amiel de Valdes. Six months later, Madame Zee changed her baptismal name to Zura de Valdes.

6 John Oliphant, *op. cit.*, p. 242.

By the end of 1931, thanks almost entirely to the hard worked imposed upon the disciples, about 10 acres of DeCourcy Island had been cleared for vegetables. There was also an orchard of fruit and nut trees. A dairy, greenhouses and a chicken house had been built, and a sawmill was established to produce their own lumber. But as the months of 1932 rolled by, Brother Twelve and Madame Zee became more and more irrational. They constantly fought with each other, and Wilson became paranoid that government forces were about to invade his islands. To repel the attackers, he had armed forts, defended by his followers, erected at strategic points.

MARY CONNALLY

In 1932 the disciples faced food rationing, hard work and mental and physical abuse far worse that they had previously endured. The situation reached a crisis when Madame Zee demanded that 78-year-old Sarah Puckett drown herself so that her spirit could return and report on the afterlife. The worsening work conditions and irrational behaviour of Brother Twelve and Madame Zee prompted the disciples to act on May 15, 1932, at which time Alfred Barley presented Wilson with a "Declaration of Independence" that had been signed by nine of the disciples.

Wilson was outraged at the revolt, and two weeks later he began to evacuate everyone from DeCourcy Island until it was deserted. The disciples responded by holding a meeting on June 5. Discussing the events of the past for the first time, they realized that they had been defrauded by Wilson and decided to seek redress through the courts. However, after initiating the proceedings through a Nanaimo lawyer, the disciples began to fear that Wilson might evoke black magic against them, and for weeks the suit was delayed. Finally, on September 24, after having been convinced that Wilson's black magic would have no effect on them,

ALFRED BARLEY

Mary Connally field a claim for $42,100, plus $10,000 in personal damages against Brother Twelve. Madame Zee was named as a co-defendant. On November 7, Alfred Barley, claiming he had been the victim of a confidence game, filed suit for $14,232.

Wilson, claiming the defendants had voluntarily given him the funds, denied all the allegations. At the trial, which began on April 26, 1933, the prosecuting attorney ran into a snag when the disciples refused to enter the witness box. They were convinced that Brother Twelve had placed a spell of black magic upon it and anyone entering it would die. It was only after reporter Bruce Mc-

The Lady Royal *lying scuttled on the beach at DeCourcy Island.*

Kelvie gave them a lip ornament, worn by an Indian woman of the Queen Charlotte Islands, and assured them it would protect them from evil spells and black magic, that each witness, clutching the charm, stepped forward to testify.

When the lawyer representing Brother Twelve and Madame Zee offered no defense to the charges, Justice Morrison awarded Mary Connally her full claim, ownership of the DeCourcy group of islands, plus 400 acres on Valdes Island. Alfred Barley was also awarded the full amount he had claimed.

But the victories won by Connally and Barley were shallow ones, since Brother Twelve and Madame Zee had fled DeCourcy Island six months earlier. Before leaving, however, they had raided the colony of Cedar and vandalized the homes.

"At the farm, houses had been pillaged and wrecked. Windows were broken, doors removed or torn from their hinges and crockery smashed against the walls. The water-tanks had been punctured by bullet holes, fruit trees were uprooted, and the farm-equipment was either missing or damaged beyond repair. In the schoolhouse, desks had been hurled out through the windows with such force that their cast-iron fillings had broken on the ground. One of the cabins had even been crushed by a huge tree felled deliberately onto its roof."[7] Brother Twelve had even scuttled the *Lady Royal* with dynamite, and she lay on her side in shallow water, vandalized and battered.

After their vandalization was complete, Brother Twelve and Madame Zee had fled across the Strait of Georgia to the Sechelt Peninsula, about 25 miles north of Vancouver. Here, in a clearing in the bush several hundred yards from the waterfront, on property purchased under the name Harold Krause, Wilson erected a comfortable cabin and the pair went into hiding. In April, 1933, shortly before the trial began, Brother Twelve and Madame Zee registered at the Empress Hotel in Victoria, where they remained during the trial.

After the trial, Brother Twelve and Madame Zee sailed to Prince

7 *Ibid*, pp. 333-334.

Rupert in the *Khuenaten*. From there they travelled by train to Montreal, then booked passage to England where they remained in hiding until August, 1934. At that time Wilson, apparently ill, decided to visit with his personal physician in Switzerland. A few months later, on November 7, 1934, Wilson died. Four days later the body was cremated and the ashes sent to his family in England. Madame Zee left Switzerland a few days later and was seldom seen or heard from again.

However, there are some who believe that Wilson faked his own death with the assistance of his doctor. John Oliphant published two intriguing accounts by Donald M. Cunliffe that tend to support this.[8] Because of the mystery surrounding the death of Edward Wilson, the whereabouts of his treasure is also a mystery.

The late Bruce McKelvie, who covered the trials and tribulations of Brother Twelve and the Aquarian Foundation, estimated that Wilson bilked his followers out of hundreds of thousands of dollars. John Oliphant records some of the larger donations in his book: Oliver Hess, $20,000; Mary Connally, $26,500; Roger Painter, over $90,000; and Alfred Barley, $14,232. The experience of one couple, Fermin and Valea Sepulveda, who left their home in California to join Brother Twelve at Valdes Island, was shared by many others. In the spring of 1931 they sold their home and all of their belongings and converted everything into cash. A week after the Sepulvedas arrived, they and other new arrivals assembled in the main meeting hall on Valdes Island where they turned over all their money to Brother Twelve. "There was a wad of bills passed out there," Valea claimed. "I never saw so much money in all my born days! That table was piled high with it, and it was all in cash."[9]

As the large sums of money continued to accumulate, Brother Twelve had it converted to American $10 and $20 gold eagles. Bruce Crawford, who did the banking for Brother Twelve, once told McKelvie that he had handled $100,000 in the Chemainus account alone, while the same was being done at Victoria and Vancouver.

"Brother Twelve continued to store his gold using the unique method he'd devised earlier. At night in the kitchen of his house at the Point, he and Madame Zee melted wax in saucepans on the cast-iron stove, while stacks of gold coins glinted in the light of the kerosene lamp. Empty mason jars stood on the table. Like alchemists in a medieval workshop, the two bent to their task, filling the jars with gold coins, then pouring melted wax into each jar. The hot paraffin flowed into the spaces around the coins, dimming their lustre as it hardened around them. Like a priest and priestess presiding over an arcane ritual, the pair repeated the procedure many times as Brother Twelve amassed a fortune in gold.

"Bruce Crawford constructed cedar boxes to hold the jars. The boxes were five inches square by nine inches deep, and a jar of gold fitted snug-

8 *Ibid*, pp. 343-346.
9 *Ibid*, p. 293.

(Above) This photo of the colony's school, which never had a scholar, was taken by Cecil Clark. Brother Twelve is believed to have stored his gold in an underground vault in the basement.
(Below) Treasure hole where Brother Twelve hid perhaps up to $500,000 in gold. This photo by Cecil Clark shows Harry Olsen lifting the concrete lid to the empty vault.

ly inside each. Brass screws held down a wooden lid, and each box was equipped with rope handles, so that despite the weight it would be easily portable. Crawford was repeatedly pressed into service, usually in the dead of night, carrying the boxes on and off the *Khuenaten*, as Brother Twelve transferred his hoard of gold from one secret cache to another. 'He would bury it in one part of the island, and then a few days later, he would dig it up again and take it to some other place,' Crawford recalled. Like a pirate captain fearful of losing his booty, Brother Twelve kept his treasure on the move, hoping to outwit a possible thief. Crawford never knew the total value of the gold, since he wasn't permitted to handle it directly, but he estimated that the sum was a substantial one, judging by the number of boxes he made—forty-three in all."[10]

Many accounts of Brother Twelve's treasure have been written over the years. Most claim the value of the treasure stood between $400,000 and $500,000. By far the most authoritative account I have read about Brother Twelve appeared in the book written by John Oliphant, from which I have quoted several times. During the course of his investigation, Oliphant located and interviewed former members of the colony, made research trips to the United States, England and Switzerland, and unearthed many rare and previously unpublished documents.

Over the years, treasure hunters have ransacked the colonists' cabins and dug holes all over Valdes and DeCourcy islands looking for the gold. Others may think part of the treasure is buried at Roberts Creek, on the Sechelt Peninsula, where Brother Twelve fled prior to the 1933 trial. Oliphant, however, claims Brother Twelve dug up all the gold before he left DeCourcy Island and took it with him to Prince Rupert. Placed in steamer trunks, it accompanied the pair to Montreal and then to England. Whether Wilson was able to spend the fortune before his "alleged" death remains a mystery. Some suggest it was placed in a Swiss bank account to which Madame Zee had access following Wilson's death. However, while there appears to be no doubt that Wilson amassed $400,000 to $500,000 in gold, there is no evidence to suggest any of it remains on DeCourcy Island. Perhaps this is best illustrated by an incident that occurred there some years later.

Mary Connally moved to DeCourcy Island after Brother Twelve and Madame Zee fled. One day Sam Greenall, her caretaker, made a unique discovery. Each time he entered the chicken house he banged his head because the floor was too high. Finally, he decided to lower it. As he did so he found a trapdoor, and no doubt thought that he had discovered one of Wilson's hiding places. Excitedly he lifted the door and peered inside. In the gloom he could make out a bundle. It turned out to be a roll of tarpaper. Greenall unrolled it and read Brother Twelve's last cryptic message. Inscribed in chalk, it read: "For fools and traitors—nothing!"[11]

10 *Ibid*, p. 306.
11 *Ibid*, p. 348.

INDEX